# reinvent yourself

# YOU
# WHO

# TODAY TOMORROW?

## reinvent yourself

tactics for work, life and happiness – yours

J. Jonathan Gabay

www.yourmomentum.com
**the stuff that drives you**

## What is momentum?

Momentum is a completely new publishing philosophy, in print and online, dedicated to giving you more of the information, inspiration and drive to enhance who you are, what you do, and how you do it.

Fusing the changing forces of work, life and technology, momentum will give you the right stuff for a brighter future and set you on the way to being all you can be.

## Who needs momentum?

Momentum is for people who want to make things happen in their careers and their lives, who want to work at something they enjoy and that's worthy of their talents and their time.

Momentum people have values and principles, and question who they are, what they do, and who for. Wherever they work, they want to feel proud of what they do. And they are hungry for information, stimulation, ideas and answers ...

## Momentum online

Visit *www.yourmomentum.com* to be part of the talent community. Here you'll find a full listing of current and future books, an archive of articles by momentum authors, sample chapters and self-assessment tools. While you're there, post your work/life questions to our momentum coaches and sign up to receive free newsletters with even more stuff to drive you.

**More momentum**

If you need more drive for your life, try one of these other momentum titles:

**soultrader**
personal career strategies for life
Carmel McConnell

**mental space**
how to find clarity in a complex life
J. Jonathan Gabay

**be your own career consultant**
how to unlock your career potential and help
yourself to your future
Gary Pyke and Stuart Neath

**managing brand me**
how to build your personal brand
Thomas Gad and
Anette Rosencreutz

**coach yourself**
make real change in your life
Anthony M. Grant and Jane Greene

**change activist**
make big things happen fast
Carmel McConnell

**lead yourself**
be where others will follow
Mick Cope

**happy mondays**
putting the pleasure back into work
Richard Reeves

**innervation**
redesign yourself for a smarter future
Guy Browning

**the big difference**
life works when you choose it
Nicola Phillips

**hey you!**
pitch to win in an ideas economy
Will Murray

**snap, crackle or stop**
change your career and create your own destiny
Barbara Quinn

**float you**
how to capitalize on your talent
Carmel McConnell and Mick Cope

**from here to e**
equip yourself for a career in the wired economy
Lisa Khoo

**grow your personal capital**
what you know, who you know and how you
use it
Hilarie Owen

PEARSON EDUCATION LIMITED

Head Office
Edinburgh Gate
Harlow CM20 2JE
Tel: +44 (0)1279 623623
Fax: +44 (0)1279 431059

London Office:
128 Long Acre, London WC2E 9AN
Tel: +44 (0)20 7447 2000
Fax: +44 (0)20 7240 5771
Website: www.yourmomentum.com

First published in Great Britain in 2002

The right of J. Jonathan Gabay to be identified as Author of this work has been asserted by him in accordance with the Copyright, Designs and Patents Act 1988.

ISBN 1843 04015 8

British Library Cataloguing in Publication Data
A CIP catalogue record for this book can be obtained from the British Library.

10 9 8 7 6 5 4 3 2

Cover and concept design by Heat.
Production design by Claire Brodmann Book Designs, Lichfield, Staffs.
Typeset by Northern Phototypesetting Co. Ltd, Bolton
Printed and bound in Great Britain by Henry Ling Ltd, Dorchester

The Publishers' policy is to use paper manufactured from sustainable forests.

## Thank you...

This book could not have been published without the support and guidance of Rachael Stock and Richard Stagg. I also thank Rachel Russell, Sandra Jones Editorial Consultant, Lesley Felce and especially Michela Rossi who initially set the wheels in motion.

Heartfelt thanks and appreciation go to my twin pillars of personal sustenance: Michelle and Joshua.

Also, to my inspirational mentor Maurice Benzimra.

This book is dedicated to Mum and Dad who provided the foundations for its entire contents.

# contents

chapter 1
re: you/ 1

chapter 2
putting your foot and mouth in it/ 11

chapter 3
the Madonna principle: reinventing your tune, image
and meaning/ 29

chapter 4
perceptions and misconceptions/ 55

chapter 5
don't dream of a revolution: realize your own
evolution/ 71

chapter 6
from knock-backs to knock-outs/ 97

chapter 7
the past, the present and you/ 121

chapter 8
following beliefs, instincts and choices/ 145

chapter 9
rebranding you/ 173

chapter 10
fit defence/ 189

chapter 11
great to see you again/ 197

chapter 12
the beginning/ 209

01

# chapter one
## re: you

reinvent yourself

Let's talk about *you*: about who that person *really* is and what that person can potentially achieve.

Every day of your life, virtually from the moment you were born, in some form or other you undergo a process of reinvention, although you may not be fully conscious of doing so. But don't worry, you are not alone.

Consider, for example, the most phenomenal reinvention process ever – the creation of the universe. Some 15 billion years ago the universe was squeezed into a super-dense state. The Big Bang explosion threw this compacted material outwards, producing the expanding universe. Through reinvention the temperature decreased, nuclei became atoms of cosmic gas and dust, nebulae *became stars* and the gases reconfigured into basic elements which fell as rain. So the initially hostile environment gradually transformed into one that could, on planet Earth at least, support life forms.

Single-cell forms evolved over millions of years into far more complex creatures called mammals. Then, after extended periods of evolution, the human ancestor that once walked on all fours, stood up on two feet. This was in accordance with a natural instinct to improve their circumstances and develop their potential. Which brings me back to you.

## A journey to you

You live in the twenty-first century but you feel you are not really 'living'. You have done it all but still feel unfulfilled.

You may have resigned yourself to being too young, too old, too set in your ways, too radical, too 'you', to take the plunge into the icy water of the reinvention pool. But believe me, you are not, and the water feels warmer than it looks.

Over the next 12 chapters join me on a voyage of discovery covering just about every important aspect of reinvention. We'll bear in mind mankind's greatest invention, the wheel, which *like your own potential*, didn't just remain stuck in the mud, but through the process of reinvention revolved intermittently, to give rise to everything from the wheelbarrow and wheelchair to micro wheel lock – used in high security technology.

Relying on the experiences of others, including my own, I'll show you ways to face up to and cope with life's realities.

## Together we'll confront what the world has to offer you, and what you can offer the world.

We'll examine why you would want to reinvent yourself in the first place. What reinvention is and, more importantly, what it isn't. Many of the topics I'll be covering will be hard-hitting, so prepare for a bumpy ride. Yet, despite this, I believe that you'll find the journey to be well worth taking.

The best place to start your fresh reinvention project is where you are *now*. It may not be a very comfortable spot. Perhaps you feel you are in the glaring spotlight, ducking the odd dropping from the sky. 'Is all this reinvention stuff just an excuse for an '*Oprah* show?' you ask. 'Is it a waste of time? Another fad destined to be shorter lived than the mini skirt?'

Give yourself a break: you deserve better. Rather than nit-picking and bemoaning about life, politics, institutions and people, do something really out of the ordinary. Not in an 'arty-farty', quick-fix, 'Mind and Body', back corner of a bookshop way. Instead, by taking small steps leading to *sustainable* changes. It's time to create your own luck. Look at your past. Recognize and accept where you've been and what you have done. After all, if you expect your world – be it the world of work or home – to treat you with respect, it makes sense to start respecting yourself.

As you watch and listen to the news about the fast-changing political, social and economic world, you may find yourself wondering what your new role is likely to become. Perhaps your work has careered off in a direction that has left you wondering whether all your efforts were really worth making. Maybe other people's promises never progressed further than the proposal stage. Or you might find yourself yearning for the days when each morning was a new challenge rather than just another day.

All these reasons and many more are healthy grounds to reinvent yourself. This book will help to make your transition a smooth one.

When I say 'healthy', I mean precisely that. Recently, a friend of mine who had struggled for much of his professional life to 'make it', phoned to tell me he had finally been promoted to his 'dream' role. 'Congratulations!' I said. 'Thanks', he replied. 'The trouble is that all the stress from worrying about whether or not I would be able to cope with it all has meant that I have had to see a psychologist! I feel like a failure even before I get to the starting block.'

I chuckled down the telephone. 'Don't you get it?' I asked. 'The mere fact that you are worried about making a change isn't an admission of failure, it's an acknowledgement that you care about your job and your new responsibilities. It also tells me that whatever your job title, you have very human qualities. And that's worth celebrating both for yourself and your future team.'

## You count

I can't promise that this book will magically improve your life or make you into an overnight success. However, it will provide the key. Which door you open is down to you.

Though this book is about you, rather than me, it's important I don't come across as a typical Agony Aunt who squints her eyes and curls her lips whilst nodding her slightly tilted head in beat to everything you say. I've been where you are. This includes having reached that crucial point in life of questioning what it's all about, and what I had become. I invite you to re-examine with me the causes of my own temporary but serious loss of direction through becoming disillusioned with people and work, which caused me to wonder how to reinvent myself. Perhaps it will help you. As it says in a book called *Growth of Ideas* (published in 1965, edited among others by Sir Julian Huxley):

People of every age stand on the shoulders of those who climbed before them. If we now live under better conditions than did men of earlier generations, if we know more and are capable of achieving more, it is because they provided us with a heritage of knowledge and ideas to build on.

Let's gather momentum by starting at the juncture where I discovered that everything had come to a grinding halt and the notion of reinvention was the last thing on my mind...

'A successful man lays a firm foundation with the bricks others have thrown at him.'

David Brinkley

## Marylebone Lane, London

In the early 1990s I was already a successful advertising agency man. But don't let that middle-class job description fool you. On the whole, times were generally good but restless. My job was to ensure that each decaying advertising campaign was replaced with another novel idea, featuring an advertised promise to reinvent someone's world into a more tolerable place. Yet, whilst I diligently worked to maintain the marketplace's vivacious love affair with hope, my own relationship with success had reached a stage where excitement was being nudged into a corner by complacency and eventually replaced by despondency.

Before I was even aware that there was a problem, success slid surreptitiously away. (As you too may have discovered, once success wanes, insecurity, anxiety and fear slither into the breach.) One morning, in despair, I took refuge in the men's loo on the first floor at the company where I worked – and cried. I was angry, bitter and cynical. I questioned everything: ethics, decency, integrity, happiness – even the meaning of life.

Maybe you too have gone through a similar experience. Perhaps you took pride at your ostensible ability to reassure work colleagues that you'll remain by their side to meet deadlines – with a veneer of supreme confidence that would make Superman or Gohan from Dragonball Z feel proud. Whilst, in truth, deep down you felt like a stand-in for Cartoon Network's *Ed, Edd n Eddy* – wondered who, if anyone, would come running to your aid when called?

Or maybe you feel tied to your work desk with just about enough space for your computer and in-tray. Or your ambition is becoming as restricted as your elbows which, if left to spread out too far, encroach into the next person's desktop territory resulting in occasional Israeli/Palestinian type disputes.

## You want to stop pushing pens and start moving forwards.

Pull over here. You can trust me – here's why:

## Big brother

To begin with, be reassured that I am not a doctor, scientist, quack or new world guru. However, in my career I have helped people re-invent brands, products, websites, training programmes, relationships, companies and aspirations. Now I want to help you.

The unifying factor in my work is that the people or teams I was working with gave the impression of being enthusiastic about their projects. I too shared their enthusiasm – well at least at first. I soon realized that in many cases, people's apparent enthusiasm was just a veneer to cover up their self interests and – even more worrying – their doubts.

You know you need to reinvent your working life when you forget what attracted you to the role in the first place. In short, when you become bored. When your hopes for something better to come along tomorrow, start to linger. Like Shirley Bassey's 'A little bit of history repeating itself'.

Although I may have had a different job title to yours, when I worked for that advertising agency, I didn't want to kick up a fuss about reinventing myself or 'the process'. I kidded myself that it was, after all, just a job and I had a life outside work. Besides when it came down to it, my ideas for actually improving, let alone reinventing matters, often made me feel like a bad karaoke act. I got 'Mmm very interesting – we'll keep those ideas on file' type of responses.

## Then became now

At my lowest point, I recalled a famous saying my secondary school teacher had quoted from Hillel (*c.* 90 BCE to 10 BCE), one of the great Jewish sages.

'If I am not for myself, who will be for me? And if not now, when?'

'If you are not for yourself, who will be for you?' refers to independence, or self-esteem. It means that people are not owned by others. It suggests that in all history there has never been, nor will there ever be, two people exactly alike with exactly the same goals. No one but you can achieve and reinvent your life purpose. Yet, everyone has the right to depend first and foremost on themselves. Then you also have to ask if being for yourself allows anyone to do whatever they fancy?

## If you are not for yourself then what are you?

I began to see the chasm between what I had so far accomplished (which at the time appeared as not that much) and what I had really wanted to achieve. I had become self-centred rather than having a sense of self.

*If not now, when?* I wondered. Despite the confusion of wondering what I could do next with my life, I was still comparatively young. If I didn't start, I would never finish – well at least not where I hoped to end up. The longer I spent wondering when to start reinventing myself, the more precious time I was wasting. I decided *there and then* on something which I invite you to take aboard *here and now*: If every moment had a purpose, mine was to reveal it – as is yours. And, through doing so, to shape your own vocation.

In this book, you will learn how to reinvent many key aspects of life both at work and at home. You'll see that your career journey can be much more rewarding than just enduring 45 minutes every morning in a crowded train – sniffing the armpits of a torso whose head is wrapped up in the daily news. Or struggling with an avalanche of in-tray and pending email requests.

You'll learn how you no longer have stay up all night worrying about striking up compromises with colleagues, friends, partners and family. In this book you will meet people who have found the supreme courage to reinvent seemingly impossible situations. Through it all, you will be able to learn from other people's mistakes and fortunes and so improve your own circumstances.

It's time to take your first steps, albeit a crawl, towards a universe of uncharted potential and untried reinvention which, like the original wheel, offers substance, not just spin.

## REINVENTING YOU

- Your entire universe is based on reinvention.

- Order comes from chaos.

- Just as you naturally crawled and then stood to walk, so you can naturally improve any given situation.

- Once you start to respect yourself, others will begin to respect you.

- Work isn't everything – your life is.

- If you are not for yourself, who will be for you?

- The time to start acting is now: the best place to start is here.

- Aim to achieve something of substance.

# chapter two
## putting your foot and mouth in it

reinvent yourself

Before you embark on your own reinvention, you need to be sure that you are doing it for your own sake rather than to impress others. Otherwise you are in danger of falling foul of that most dreadful disease involving putting your foot in your mouth namely, BSE (Become Someone Else). Like many infections, BSE proliferates from the head down. The 'powers' at the top urge you to fly high. The posters on the street corners promise that you can fly far. The Hollywood feel-good movies urge you to fly solo.

In the real world, *your* world, if on the off-chance your feet should rise too far off the ground for most people's insecurities, you had better BSE. Become Someone who fits more snugly into other people's lives.

This striving to be identified with someone else, in order to please those who manipulate lives in one way or another, is often mistaken for the pursuit of reinvention. Many change themselves in order to please others, kidding themselves that if they can be accepted according to their peers' standards of what is 'Best Standards' compliant, then they will be acknowledged for who they truly are.

Of course, this is ridiculous. People just end up trying to become who and what they assume others probably want them to be. Everyone ends up mimicking each other, rather than valuing themselves; using those 'Best Practice Standards' whose original authorship remains anonymous.

$$R = C^2$$

**(Reinvention = Collaboration + Communication)**

So, what's stopping *you* reinventing? For starters, probably people whose vested interests lie in keeping you where and how you are. Don't blame them entirely, seek rather to understand. Maybe their motives for self-preservation are not that different from yours. By collaborating rather than conflicting, the chances are strong that they can benefit as well from reinvention.

'To lead the people, walk behind them.'

Lao-Tzu, sixth century BC

It is hardly surprising then that today, especially at the workplace, many well-intentioned reinventors have become nothing more than the re-processed. Rather than running their own lives they allow everyone else to run it for them. Daily, as they comb their hair in the company's washroom, they chant, 'Tomorrow I'll change it all.' But, come tomorrow, all is back to 'normal'.

## Become the king of rock rather than 'beg and roll over'

One of the most notorious cases of BSE relates to Elvis Presley, a truly outstanding singer. Yet, after his death, despite having millions of adoring fans, it was widely reported that the 'The King' was incredibly lonely. Sadly, much of the loneliness was attributed to the person who had helped to make him famous in the first place, namely his manager, Colonel Tom Parker. As Larry Geller, a close friend of Elvis's, explained:

Whilst Elvis loved to sing, he also wanted to act – in 'serious' movies, not just 'B' movies. It's astonishing that a man as famous as Elvis was so tightly controlled in every aspect of his life by Parker … Towards the end Elvis confided in me that one day he hoped to dismiss Parker. It was definitely a control thing.

So it seems that even the brightest, most talented stars can remain in the dark when it comes to challenging people to whom they feel obligated for having once given them a lucky break.

Of course, apart from any consideration of common courtesy and basic human decency, it's sensible to acknowledge the help received along your reinvention journey through life; assuming that you build on any opportunity you have been given. If, on the other hand, you choose to remain in someone else's shadow, perhaps out of a sense of guilt, then there you will remain, as one of life's spectators rather than players.

## The first rule of reinvention is to decide on your goals – on your own terms.

Then, even if you don't achieve all of them, you will have the satisfaction of knowing that like another 'king of music' during Elvis's era, you did it *your way*.

## Cling on to what you believe

People who hang on to a celebrity's coat tails in the hope of reinvention 'rubbing off' on them, are common in every walk of life. Even more prevalent are those who struggle to reach a certain peak. Once that plateau has been attained, they adamantly refuse to move on to a higher level. Often this is simply because they feel that the world ought to stop and pay tribute to their wonderful feats to date. This is ridiculous. It's like a hamburger company saying, 'Well, twenty years ago we introduced the hamburger. Despite the fact that our competitors now also offer cheeseburgers and veggie-burgers, there's no need to modify our service in anyway. After all we are just too wonderful to worry about such trivial matters.'

Countless instances abound of those who acquire their '15 minutes of fame' (as promised by Andy Warhol), then find the limelight is quickly dimmed by reality. Don't make the classic mistake of former 'A' list celebrities now content to languish in the 'C' or even 'D' list category, who spend the rest of their lives vainly trying to recapture their glory-days rather than moving on to face new challenges. You can spot them in any afternoon television game show still cracking the same old gags which a once famous middle-aged host still finds funny.

# Aim at stretching your 15 minutes of fame into a lifetime of success.

For these people – including the familiar ones whom you meet in your everyday personal and business life – reinvention grinds to a halt. No doubt you know a middle manager who peaked years ago, yet clung so desperately to his career ascendancy that he forgot to move on.

## Make a move

It reminds me of the frog who spent his life squatting on a leaf in the middle of the pond near a volcano. He became so accustomed to his position that he didn't even bother leaping to catch flies. When the other frogs called from different parts of the pond and even beyond about new feeding and breeding grounds he would simply stick his neck up high and sneer at them. As for food, he perfected the art of licking flies from the air with a flick of his elongated tongue – without having to disturb his square-footing.

One day the volcano erupted and the water in the pond started to boil. The frog's feet scorched yet he still would not move. Ultimately he died, steamed alive. Yet to prevent that fate, all he had to do was to take not so much as a giant leap into the unknown, but a gentle hop to safer ground.

Often people turn to reinvention when it's too late to plan ahead. It becomes an escape rather than an adventure. For you, positive reinvention should be an ongoing process of self-improvement rather than driving yourself into different corners (or allowing others to drive you into them.) If you don't make the move to new ground – at the right time – your colleagues will, leaving you behind to rehash rather than reinvent and improve your talents.

## Blink and it's over

Today's celebrity status has an incredibly short duration. According to most of the gossip press, once fame is achieved, even the most renowned celebrities spend their careers aiming to reinvent themselves in a desperate game of trying to second-guess what's going to be 'in' before their fans vote them 'out'.

In an interview, Robbie Williams, former member of Take That and an international pop icon in his own right, said after several successful albums, 'I'm bored with Robbie. I haven't decided what the new style will be.' It was a typical comment from a man notorious for shadow dancing with reinvention.

Ironically, according to many psychologists, many featured celebrities in the showbiz and lifestyle magazines spend most of their time trying to ensure that their performances on and off screen, stage and wherever else that they have earned their reputation, closely matches the lives of their adoring fans – you and me. Which begs the question, 'Who's copying who?'

## Don't do as I do. Do as I say.

Part of my job is to lecture on advertising and marketing and teach MBAs. My aim throughout is to apply Confucius's maxim: 'One does not preach what he practises until he practises what he preaches.' As well as:

## 'Find a job you love and you'll never have to work a day in your life.'

Some years ago I discovered in conversation with tutors from various colleges that it was not uncommon to hear students asking for expert advice on issues of 'best practice' in one area or another. When the tutors didn't know, they would make up the answer! Providing it sounded relatively plausible, most got away with it. So much so, that their make-do advice would eventually be recorded in journals as 'Best Practice' gospel. (Hallelujah!)

## From reinventing people to reinventing processes

Take the story of one guy with a great gift for number crunching. This fellow was so good at maths that during his adolescence whilst others were giggling in the back row of the movies, he was chuckling to himself about the beauty of how numbers could be made to create highly complex patterns. (Between you and me I always suspected the guy was a bit weird!)

He went on to run courses on business management and accountancy. One day a trade magazine asked him to write up a piece about the mathematical problems and opportunities affecting the average international warehousing firm, arising through distribution and the Internet. He wrote up his theory whilst on a long train journey. However, in an act of total mischievousness, he made sure that although the theory sounded impressive, in truth the entire article was a total myth based on elaborate yet unfounded conjecture!

He half-wanted the editor of the magazine to spot the gibberish. Yet it was passed for publication. Several years later, he attended a seminar on warehouse distribution and to his amazement, the speaker was referring to his article as the 'best practice' procedure to be adopted by any serious-minded warehousing manager wishing to reinvent current processes. His myth had become a legend!

## Give people something to believe in

I question whether this cavalier 'who cares where it comes from – providing it sounds alright' attitude – is a responsible not to say ethical way to help people reinforce or reinvent processes. Nevertheless, at risk of being the one who announces that the Emperor is in fact not wearing any clothes, I have to admit that in all aspects of the commercial world, the tactic is commonplace. The 'gospel' earns even greater credence if endorsed by others within the same respected circle. (You may be more familiar with this kind of thing as 'the old boy network'.)

Given the chance to believe in something, provided it is appropriately marketed and appears to confirm values and views, most people are happy to accept practically any type of advice. Which is why I teach my own students the importance of responsibility of truth toward the customer, the business, the network and above all themselves.

## Become the centre of everything

Credibility, and by implication, gravitas, is often attained when ideas are endorsed by key people – although not necessarily practised. Consequently, these central people collaborate within a tight circle of key associates who know other people with similar interests. In this way, the close-knit circle links to a number of smaller work units or social circles, which in turn collectively link to many more circles touching at their perimeter ever-broader interested parties. Each consequential circle of people carries the message of an idea to others, lending their interpretation to the original idea and so oiling the 'spin' which keeps the circles revolving and message spreading even wider to more distant communities. In so doing, they play their role in the swelling process of influencing people to accept an idea.

In other words:

'Take it from me, you can believe this guy.'

*'Why?'*

'Because I heard from someone in the know that he knows his stuff.'

*'Who?'*

'Well, between you and me, let's just say it was someone who's in the right place. If you know what I am saying.'

*'Ah yes, knowing the person "in the know" I know where you are coming from.'*

*'I somehow I guessed you would.'*

Take as an example a '20-something' year-old IT manager who chews over the thought that in terms of life opportunities, even his pc has more bytes than him. So, he decides to change the odds in his favour. First, rather than standing on the edges of his business community, he positions himself in the centre of his network of friends and acquaintances who could carry his ideas towards the wider market. Providing those ideas are based on substance rather than just hype, he can look forward to eventually becoming the source of innovation. (It takes guts for the IT manager to start such a process rolling, yet through doing so, he can feel assured that he is no longer being taken for granted.)

## One man's 'reality' is another's ridicule

Often people dream to change the world but, through frustration, end up changing their minds. Not because they are pessimists but because in their eyes at least, they believe they are realists.

One of the many dangers of prevaricating reinvention is that the forces of the unholy trinity of Complacency, Mediocrity and Suspicion conspire to shorten your long-sighted optimism.

## For every person climbing the ladder of success, there are hundreds more waiting to catch the elevator.

Through procrastination, by the time you arrive at where you want to be – the centre of everything – you could find yourself at the hollow hub of nothing. Wishing to do the 'correct thing', you want to defend the rights of your team and the honour of your hard-grafted achievements. You want to be the kind of manager that you always hoped for – considerate but firm. You want to be the kind parent that 'does the right thing' for your kids. Yet you feel you are facing a brick wall of doubt, rather than climbing a mountain of promise. It needn't be that way.

## To you it's a mental block – to the reinventor it's art

Getting people to believe in you is especially difficult if all you can see is a big block barring your progress. My advice is to visualize the fears preventing you from moving on as a vast block of ice. Now imagine that you are an ice-sculptor. You are commissioned to craft a beautiful peacock from a massive mound of ice. Rather than chipping in shapes to resemble the bird, chip *out* anything that doesn't look like the bird. The more you chip at your fears, the closer you'll get to discovering that you probably already have the core ingredients to become fulfilled– and probably always had.

Leaping over the hurdles of fear takes courage and determination. The greatest strength of all is the determination to do what you believe in spite of any uncertainties and worries.

Being afraid is natural. Most people who decide not to stretch their full potential by settling for next to nothing of what often turns out to be not that much in the first place, are scared. So too are major risk takers like entrepreneurs. The only difference between people who take big risks and those who don't take chances is that at least those who took the plunge to change things had a legitimate reason to be scared in the first place.

'When you come to the end of your rope, tie a knot and hang on.'
Franklin D. Roosevelt

Right now you may think that you are lost – maybe in a job that offered so much initially but delivered so little. But take a good long look at the spot you're standing on. You are on *terra firma*. Desperate or bleak as it may seem, that place is probably the best position from where to proceed. Experience, circumstance and luck – good or ghastly – have landed you at this particular spot since you had to cross, stumble and leap over various hurdles. If you feel lost or stuck in a rut at work or at home, this knowledge is essential. Hold on to it.

You have a ready-made market that, through your efforts, can be amplified. As a reinventor, exploit it.

To a great extent, exploiting reinvention calls for you to reach out for what you want and deserve, both mentally as well as physically. Just grabbing anything that may pass your way leaves too much to chance. On the other hand, purely planning reinvention in your mind and never actually being brave enough to do anything about it physically is the stuff of daydreams. 'Doing' rather than purely deliberating will extend your influence – however great or modest – to another circle of like-minded people, who in turn may offer you support or combine their resources to widen your reach. It's all too easy to be frozen by inertia. So much so, that when it comes to having to motivate yourself, progress can be as slow as waiting for an enormous glacier to melt.

## Stand apart but not at a distance

Perhaps reaching out means standing up for yourself as an individual who opposes one fixed system (such as the one at work) in order to develop and promote a fresh one of your own making and style. This might entail venturing out to freelance or changing your employer. The drawback with this approach is that unless you can socialize with new contacts even at the most humble levels – and so be considered a part of the intended circle that you are trying to influence – you'll never develop enough influence to attract would-be dissidents to your new circle. As Rudyard Kipling would have put it, you need to 'talk with crowds, whilst keeping your virtue, as well as walk with Kings, without losing the common touch'.

Building confidence to establish your individuality, whilst securing established links does not need to be a traumatic affair. Often it starts with subtle changes which, in time grow into acceptance. It's a bit like wearing a trendy pair of Nike, Puma, Reebok or Adidas sneakers that anyone who is anyone in your social or working community wants to be seen in.

Stylistically, your shoes are basically no different to those worn by the other members of your community, except for a discreet variation on the inside lining stitching and laces. That is your variation, your theme, your groove, your uniqueness, which allows you to individualize the way you want to live your life. Who knows? Eventually everyone who is anyone will want to be stepping into your shoes – *you* would have BSE'd *them*.

## Reinvention at Web-speed

The Internet revolution, often publicized by sneaker-footed would-be millionaires, promised to reinvent futures virtually overnight. For some business people and 'techies' who would have otherwise been fated to live out their lives munching on take-away pizza and writing codes of data, the promise fulfilled itself. In the broader world, the Internet offered unrivalled access to information and so choice.

Yet, the choice of access to information, products and services became obscured by promises of even greater riches. When macho corporate sponsors of major media networks asked what else the general public wanted the Internet to be, the question was often misinterpreted as what they (including yourself) wanted to personally become.

In the rush for a quick solution, many contenders sacrificed what they had for what they thought would be given rather than earned through considered reinvention. As the Nasdaq index collapsed it became apparent that such overnight transformations are rarely sustainable.

For many like Gail, the '20-something' IT project manager who once worked for an Internet company which specialized in information systems, reinvention meant more than just slick Web promises. Gail got into high tech by chance…

I wanted to work with people, not in front of a computer screen all day. An employment agency suggested I call a company looking for a specialist engineer. They gave me a break.

The work was interesting and in the beginning the pressure was positive. However, the hours were too long. I worked there for two and half years, but if you figure in all the overtime, it was more like three and a half years. If I wanted to leave early I had to find an excuse, as if I was doing something wrong.

I didn't understand my co-workers. They were people who got married, went off on a fancy honeymoon and then came back and worked all day and night. From my point of view it was slave labour. When I got home at night I had no strength to cook, so I ate out. I used to spend a fortune on clothes and appearances so that I would feel I was getting something after all the work.

It took me two years to realize that life was passing me by, although I knew I would earn much less in any other job and that scared me. But after the shares began to fall, I was out of there. It was time to return to the sane world.

Now Gail works in an accountancy practice with no special perks such as mobile phones and car.

'I'll be studying for an MA in philosophy – as far away from high tech as you can get. To high tech people who have been given the boot, I have one thing to say: This is a once in a lifetime opportunity. Start living for yourselves and not for others.

Just as Gail reinvented her dream rather than promises made by would-be Web entrepreneurs whose businesses ultimately went from dot coms to not coms, so it makes sense for you to pursue your own path.

## Follow the Yellow Brick Road

You are the final arbiter of which path to follow. Contrary to the clichéd image, although your road to success is still under construction, that road is neither long or lonesome. In fact, it's one of literally hundreds of thousands featured in your personal map of life. Choosing the right road is often influenced by who has previously travelled along it. So it makes sense to watch and learn from other people's journeys. This doesn't mean that once you choose a direction in life you always have to stick with it just because others have done so already.

# Your life map is forever being drawn-up and you are the cartographer.

Sometimes you may find a companion on your chosen route who helps support you along the way. Other times you may decide to take the next crossroads away from those with whom you no longer find any kinship. And at other times still, you may want to follow completely different directions pioneered by people whom you admire.

We all need each other to expand the richness and diversity of our lives. The people with whom you collaborate can help you build, step by step, brick by brick, your own utopian Yellow Brick Road.

However, the substance which cements your chosen path is as solid as the amount of effort you put into believing in yourself, supported by your determination to achieve your chosen goals.

Every now and then, just as you begin to find courage to believe in yourself through kick-starting a reinvention project, others who are probably envious of your new-found inner strength, try to put you off-track by removing the odd brick or two.

## Home goal

Take the legendary English footballer David Beckham. Playing for Manchester United, he put up with incessant criticism from literally thousands of football followers, as well as fashion critics and the media commenting on every detail of his life from his choice of haircut to weighing up social prospects for his wife.

Then there were the academics who probed into Beckham's intelligence levels, including the zealots who debated over whether he should represent the homeland of the Church of England at Sunday football matches. At times it seemed that 'everyone and his dog' stoked up the fire of dissatisfaction and gossip that produced a steady stream of hot air around his incontrovertibly dazzling football skills.

Gossip is like a film. It begins with a negative, then is developed and often enlarged. In the face of such open hostilities, Beckham could have easily given up on the whole sordid business of football and retire on the considerable wealth he had already accumulated. Instead, he did something quite extraordinary. Ignoring the jibes and whistles from the terraces, Beckham searched within himself and reinvented his attitude and temperament which with his innate talent took him to international sporting eminence, culminating with captaincy of the English team.

You can be sure that along Beckham's road, though some football commentators, fans of other clubs, journalists and others removed bricks all over the place, undoubtedly there were people who helped him over the rocky patches. As you dig inside for that internal change you want to make, so look around you for the support to do it.

## Rise to the top

Another sporting champion, Dr Tenley Albright, the Olympic Gold Medal figure skater said, 'When you go flat on your face sliding across the ice, there is only one thing to do … get up and try again.'

Trying again a different way takes determination cemented with confidence. The kind of guts which everyone, in any career who believes in meritocracy, has the right to show with pride. For example, when it comes to battling for prime positions at the workplace, everyone has the right to be seen and eventually judged as individual contenders whose abilities in terms of knowledge, skills and confidence help them rise to the top of a heap of CVs.

Moving ever onwards and upwards, and adapting as you go, calls for zeal, character, charisma, enthusiasm and integrity. Above all, it demands the will and determination to reinvent a tired process – one originally intended to impress your current or potential boss – to move you in a new direction. This perfectly fits the ideal of innovative reinvention.

Let's turn to the next chapter. In doing so I hope to spin you from a virgin apprentice winner to a saintly victor – singing your own tune.

## REINVENTING YOU

- Aim at stretching your 15 minutes of fame into a lifetime of success.

- Strive to become the source of reinvention, rather than the receptor of it.

- Face fear and follow your beliefs.

- Don't be afraid of taking risks.

- Turn what you know into what you can achieve.

- For every person climbing the ladder of success there are hundreds more waiting to catch the elevator.

- Stand apart – but not at a distance.

- Become you – not someone else.

- Collaborate with people whom you trust.

- If you fall, get back up again.

- Follow your own instincts, rather than relying totally on others.

- Walk in confidence rather than dance to cynicism.

- Don't let reinvention become displaced by discouragement.

- Don't just plan, start your reinvention process.

- Don't give up anything – just enhance what you already have.

- Create your own luck.

03

# chapter three

## the Madonna principle: reinventing your tune, image and meaning

reinvent yourself

For me, Madonna, hailed by British fans at concerts chanting, 'God Save *our* Queen', has always been the epitome of reinvention. Around the world, initially young girls, teens, then adults have consistently cited the pop diva as the definitive role model on how best to reinvent oneself. Other pop divas like Geri Halliwell and Kylie Minogue also seem to shape their reinvention upon the mother of all image reinventors.

Madonna Louise Veronica Ciccone started her career selling donuts in New York's Times Square. She went on to be regarded variously as a Virgin Mary figure, Catholic sinner, horny teaser, disco diva, techno gigahead, earth matriarch, right-on sister, bell-buttoned ragdoll, resurrected Monroe, prima donna Peron, Zen-driven fitness fanatic, atomic war-head armed, nipple-busting, hot-wired, breast-plated sexual liberator, gay 'Vogue' dancing queen, bawdy cowgirl, savvy magnate, naïve bride, MTV three-minute boiled flick-chick, championing campaigner, fantasy middle-class 'Reader's Wives' aged 40 something homemaker … the list is still being reinvented as she remains a work in progress.

Yet those who follow her trends for the most part end just there, *following* and trying to catch up. Whilst Madonna continues to set new fashions for others to follow, those who fail probably confuse success for notoriety. Whilst success brings good fortune, notoriety tends to conjure up curses.

Real success isn't measured by how many times you can spot your name in the press or company intranet. It's more to do with how long you can look confidently at yourself in the mirror feeling contented with your lot and optimistic about your qualities.

Ever since one of her first international best-selling songs (*Like a Virgin*) hit the charts, along with most other young male adults with more verve than nerve, I bought into the idea that Madonna – with a highly publicized reputation for being sexually liberal – was indeed a virgin!

In other words, how did Madonna consistently present an image of one kind of person, whilst many supposed or even wanted to believe that she was something else? More intriguingly still, when it comes to it, do you present to the world different images than the ones you picture of yourself and why?

In terms of Madonna's image, I am not sure that she has ever been anyone other than herself. She held this view in an interview to Elle magazine: 'I hate this obsession people have about me reinventing myself. For me it's all about revealing. I keep on taking off the layers.'

Assuming that is true, Madonna displays layers of what she has always been. Each 'reveal' is just a different aspect of the same person. Edward de Bono discussed a similar notion in his book, *Six Thinking Hats*. He argued that the best way to tackle a problem isn't head on, but using your head. Each situation calls for a different approach or 'hat'. You simply deal with each circumstance in the most logical or appropriate way.

Madonna seems to have developed this idea and turned it upside down. Rather than putting on a new 'hat' for each occasion, she simply reveals another hitherto latent facet of herself from her extensive anthology. In so doing, she exposes a further unfamiliar aspect rather than presenting something that is already known but renovated to appear new.

That takes guts. Most people are uncomfortable about revealing themselves to the world. It's long been this way.

reinvent yourself

## The fruits of knowledge

In the book of Genesis, it is explained that God created Adam and Eve naked. This was no big deal to the couple. It was only after eating from the forbidden tree of knowledge that they felt exposed, and in Adam's words, 'afraid'. They even went as far to try to hide themselves from their Creator, amongst the trees in the Garden of Eden – a pretty dumb exercise as he was all-knowing.

With the exception of dimensions and cosmetic tweaks, in the most part beneath our clothes – even those of the designer-labelled variety – we are all equal. As the great American novelist, Mark Twain put it, 'We are all alike on the inside'. Yet, we maintain a fear of exposing ourselves. All this is certainly not leading to the suggestion that you should fling off your clothes at the next management meeting as part of an expression of sexual and social liberation!

However, it is interesting to analyze what makes us so ashamed, even fearful of exposing what lies beneath the various shades and hues that we use as protective veneers. Perhaps we are so fervent in our need for people to believe that we are what we present to the world that we delude ourselves into thinking that the facade is the naked truth of what we believe, as opposed to the bare facts of what we really have become.

**As the former Israeli Premier, the late Golda Meir put it, 'Don't be humble. You're not that great.'**

## You are a person – not a label

I recently watched a television programme on British TV called *Could you Live without Designer Labels?* It featured an upper-class family (mum, dad, son and daughter) from Manchester, England. They agreed to forgo for a week their designer trinkets and marques, including Mercedes cars and French fashion label clothes.

At first, the entire family were aghast at the prospect of ditching their *'glam rags'* and accessories, like Italian handbags, for *'glad rags'*, such as shell suits bought from the local open-air market. Mum was shocked to discover that she would not be allowed home niceties like a tin of Heinz baked beans. Instead, she would have to open a tin of bargain basement baked beans. 'There's no way I'm touching this stuff. A bean is not a bean unless it's from Heinz.' Yet, as the days passed, Mum and daughter began not just to accept their challenge but to relish it.

However, for Dad, it was all too much. For example, he had to drive the family in a Vauxhall Vector car to their local bistro frequented by friends who were more accustomed to seeing him pull up in a top of the range company Merc. 'This isn't a car', declared the young son pointing to the Vauxhall Vector. 'It's just a lump of metal to get you from A to B!'

Towards the end of the week, Dad couldn't put up with the challenge any longer. In the spirit of the maxim that 'money doesn't talk, it swears', he simply *had* to buy an Armani tie. 'Why did you do it?', asked his wife. 'Look, I've had a bloody awful day in the City, I deserve it', snapped back the flustered husband. Interestingly enough, at that point, the wife began to see her husband in a different light.

As the experiment drew to a close, the Mercs, clothes and various designer trinkets were returned. Upon seeing scores of storage boxes containing dozens of pairs of shoes, a huge collection of dresses, tops and so forth, the wife realized that rather than enhance her appearance, all the clothes had managed to achieve before was to suppress what she really felt about herself.

Thanks in part to the media message that material reinvention can be easily financed on credit, this kind of thing could happen to anyone chasing the all star-spangled European / Australian / American / Express dream. The trouble is that their chattels may become a habit that is increasingly costly to sustain.

## Wear reinvention on your sleeve

Madonna, unlike the woman in the TV programme, rather than using money to envelop insecurities, used it to buy high-fashion clothes that proclaimed her philosophy. This kind of thinking is often adopted by companies which want to present a uniformed (literally) image of their workforce. Yet, however elegantly designed those uniforms may appear, the people who breathe, walk and talk beneath the fibre thickness glamour still have to assert themselves as individuals as opposed to assuming the roles of anthropomorphic clothes horses.

If I were asked to market success as a product, I would ensure that the label appears on the outside so everyone would see it at face value. Yet, the core of what success means can only be appreciated by the people who look beyond the façade and see what's inside.

## Aim at revealing – in your own good time – layers of who you really are.

Likewise as Madonna matures and discovers new independent views about the way she reacts to her world and what that world needs, so she reveals corresponding layers which people tend either to love or hate. Either way, she is doing things *on her terms*. For many of her fans, especially women, that is really empowering as well as highly motivating.

Arguably, to reinvent yourself successfully, like Madonna, it makes sense to develop into your own brand consultant. It's yet another tactic which leading global companies take very seriously indeed.

Consider whether you would be brave enough to look at who you are and, like Madonna, adapt aspects of the multi-layered facets of yourself to complement your environment as opposed to trying to change it completely. Or like the family in the TV programme, preferring to become an image as opposed to wearing your heart on your sleeve?

In other words, could you stand up to being simply you? In Madonna's own words, her project goals have been 'to be revolutionary, in a quiet way'. (I'll delve further into this in a later chapter – 'Rebranding You'.)

'The wise do not judge others' words or deeds or what they have or have not done. The wise one only contemplates their own words and deeds.'

Buddha

To embrace courage, confidence and commitment to take control of your outward appearance to the world, you will need the coolness to believe in yourself. First you must acknowledge who and what you are – good, bad, beautiful or downright ugly.

Having such confidence, without becoming arrogant, should further encourage you to reveal yourself to the people whom previously you suspected for judging you wrongly. Having exposed yourself for who and what you are, you will still need to remove those rose-tinted glasses to recognize those still choosing to pre-judge you. It doesn't mean that you have lost respect for them or that you should belittle your own achievements nor indeed theirs.

Honesty is one of the hardest aspects of the reinvention process. It is widely recognized that in her mission to reinvent herself, Madonna made lots of commercial 'enemies'. This goes with the territory when you are being true to yourself rather than a hollow echo of how you think someone else sees you.

I am not suggesting that you should become a complete autonomous maverick. Unless, of course, it doesn't bother you that people may befriend you one day and ignore you the next. It's *your* life and your own reinvention process. However, until you openly accept what and who you are, you stand no chance of being received as part of a wider group of advocates utterly believing in themselves and generating confidence and self-assurance to those surrounding them.

You could argue that it didn't matter a jot to Madonna that she made enemies on her path towards reinvention. After all, she could literally afford to make enemies, friends or acquaintances with whomsoever she pleased. Perhaps. What did concern her, was to ensure that whichever side of herself she chose to reveal at any point, it would turn out to be the most gratifying.

Clearly, Madonna struggled and worked hard to achieve the ideal image: as if it were the most important project in the world. If at a practical level she wanted to reveal a mystical characteristic, Madonna would invest the time and effort necessary to ensure that her clothes, make-up and general appearance were as authentic to true mysticism as she considered appropriate.

This reminds me of a highly provocative poster advertisement for Afghan carpets. It showed a person at prayer on his knees, face bowed low, looking at the carpet. The headline read 'Allah is in the details'. In terms of reinvention that is true to your values and beliefs, *you* are 'in the detail'.

'The greatest danger for most of us is not that our aim is too high and we miss it, but that it is too low and we reach it.'

Michelangelo

Which brings me neatly to the question of projects. Your reinvention is never an end in itself. It is an ongoing process of links within a chain. You know the old saying that any chain is only as strong as its weakest link. So it follows that it pays big dividends to work on small projects – the current link in your own chain of reinvention missions.

In the instance of a mystical image, Madonna cultivated every detail like the intricacy of the henna designs which adorned her hands on MTV videos. So it is that the smaller your own project the better.

At work, many tend to whine about not being given 'a big enough project'. Worst still, they moan that working on the smallest aspect of an on-going project which has been active for months isn't as satisfying as getting to grips with bigger schemes. This is nonsense. Little projects are part of your on-going life apprenticeship in understanding how to make the most of your ability – and take it farther. In fact, just as a life is made up of small, yet not trivial events, so without small projects, greater achievements can never be reached.

## Your starter for ten

Consider the case of the 1970s British television quiz show, *University Challenge*. The quiz-master, Bamber Gascoigne, meticulously revised the questions as well as answers of every quiz. So much so that he would research what would likely be given as the *wrong answer*. If such an answer were presented, Gascoigne would say, 'Bad luck. You were almost right. You must have been thinking of "such and such" (his researched alternative) – an easy mistake to make.'

All other quiz masters just read whatever was on their card. Gascoigne, however, cultivated an art form for understanding the small details. The result? One of the most successful and enduring quiz shows on British television.

## Nothing works better than a hard-working reinventor

A five-year piece of research of leading exponents in fields such as athletics, the arts and academia, conducted by Dr Benjamin Bloom of the University of Chicago, concluded that the only characteristic shared by the cream of the crop was a commitment to hard work, supported by extraordinary drive and determination.

It's like the story often told about the artist Michelangelo. A man pointed out to Michelangelo the lack of progress in his paintings. Michelangelo retorted, 'If you really look carefully you will see that I have slightly polished this bit and softened a few lines here.' 'Yes – but those are trifles!' laughed the man. 'Perhaps,' replied Michelangelo, 'but trifles make perfection and perfection is no trifle.'

## To reinvent the bigger picture, start looking at the small details.

You need to change not just what you do, but the way you do it, based on an understanding of why you should – or perhaps should no longer – follow a particular direction.

# Bit by bit, not bite by chew

During my career, I have worked on behalf of several leading charities, promoting worthy causes and hopefully raising cash. In every case I have followed the rule that if you present a potential 'man in the street' donor with a disaster scenario on a vast scale such as an earthquake, world poverty, disease and so on, little cash is raised.

However, if you present the same problems in bite-sized chunks, the results differ dramatically; such as highlighting the plight of one community whose homes have been lost through an earthquake. Or giving a poor family a donation for just five pounds towards a humble business venture, or towards the cost of a trip to the seaside for a child with leukaemia.

The logic of this reminds me of the *Guinness Book of Records* which documents the legendary achievement of a Frenchman called Michel Lotito. He ate a whole bicycle! However, he didn't scoff the lot at one sitting! Between 17 March and 2 April 1977, Lotito melted the parts into 'petite' pieces and swallowed them.

# So what is it you want to reinvent?

Before your take a big 'gulp' at the prospect, let me reassure you that your reinvention project could take the form of many other guises. The project needn't even be of the Madonna-type glamour variety.

◆ Maybe you are fed up with being ignored.

◆ Maybe you are sick and tired of being the centre of attention when all you really want is to be accepted as one of the 'guys'.

◆ Maybe you know you need to find more time for home life but are too scared of the repercussions on your business.

◆ Maybe you have watched your boss and thought, 'I could do the job better'.

- Maybe you wish your relationship with a partner could be as fresh as it was when you first met, but find it too difficult to escape the roles that you've grown into.

- Maybe you want to find some time to do your own thing – for no other reason than having a break from the office and its politics for a while.

- Maybe you've ended up in a situation where those you love, or even work with, are frustrated by your anger towards them which, in reality, is directed at yourself.

- Maybe you feel that organizational procedures or regulations don't make good bedfellows with fundamental justice.

- Maybe you want a better reason to get out of bed in the morning than going to work to make your boss look good.

- Maybe you need a break from being the 'perfect' parent, worker, lover …

- Maybe you know you are not doing yourself any favours, but it's easier than having to face reality.

- Maybe you want to feel there is more to your daily routine than watching morning tv, spending the afternoon window shopping, and the early evening cooking the dinner for someone who honestly believes you care about their frustrating day in the office.

- Maybe you are bored with listening to the same old stories at lunchtime from work colleagues.

- Maybe you would like to look through a window rather than at the Windows operating system all day long.

- Maybe you are no longer in the mood to offer a cheery 'Did you have a nice weekend?' smile on Monday mornings.

- Maybe you wish your life were as orderly and vibrant as your 'alleged' life neatly summed up on your single-sided A4 curriculum vitae.

◆ Maybe you want to stop wondering about 'maybes' but can't seem to think any further.

Maybe it's time for *you*.

## Approaches to reinvention

Individual reinvention projects can be very small indeed. Take as an example, arranging a new kind of rota to pick up the kids from school, to give you more time or to make life less stressful, or planning a different kind of customer assessment worksheet at the office, as part of your whole job reinvention.

Let's consider separately both projects and see how the outcome can be applied as part of your daily reinvention process.

First, that rota to pick up the kids from school: Time pressures may be immense, and the kids may become irritable at your rushing about. That could lead them to being uncooperative and so on – it all adds to that old pressure pot!

So what could you do about it? Bit by bit, consider your options.

1 *Grin and bear it and just get on with it*
   You could throw your problems in the air and hope that they will fall back to earth in the right order. If nothing else, this approach certainly shows a great deal of optimism and you could get lucky. However, your reinvention is too important to rely on luck alone.

2 *Lateral thinking*
   How about being tangential in your thinking, rather like those 'Six Thinking Hats' referred to earlier? Lateral thinking encourages you to consider new, often wacky options. For example, to save time picking up the kids from school, why not give up your job and teach them at home? I am joking. And that's often the problem related to lateral thinking. You allow your

mind to wander, but you may end up with just a long list of mostly useless innovations.

**3** *The unilateral interrogation method*
You examine in fine detail just one aspect of your project and never let it go. Then you put that issue under a spotlight and begin to probe even further, digging deeper and deeper. For example, saving time.

I need to save time
I could drive faster
Better buy a faster car
Better change my job to earn more money for the faster car
HELP! Dig me out of this hole!

## Stretch your thinking and you'll expand your potential.

How about combining the best of all methods into an idea which I call the Three-Way Technique (TWT)? TWT is based on the premise that tackling problems in isolation hardly ever provides even a partial solution.

You are facing the issue – picking the kids up from school – by taking up your option of flexitime at work. On your left are all the factual aspects of your issue which have landed you in the current situation. On your right are all your available options. Sandwiched between the two is a series of creative suppositions bridging the gap.

## Three-Way Technique at a glance

◆ Consider the facts which got you where you are, step by step.

◆ Where would you like to end up? Rather than doing things just a touch better, imagine where in a perfect world, ideally you would like to be.

- Based on your knowledge, what are your options?

- Use those considered options and findings to effect changes.

- Rather than drown yourself in a sea of knowledge, constantly remind yourself that you are swimming towards land – a place of opportunities – but don't splash about, use your key findings to propel you further.

- Finally, use those considered options and findings by way of reinvention, perhaps not ending up where you first ideally wanted, but arriving at a more rewarding land of opportunity.

Reverting to the issue of picking up the kids from school:

- *TWT stage one*
  Could you picture yourself meeting other parents next time you pick up your child?

- *TWT stage two*
  Could you befriend some of the other parents? Could their children befriend yours, so expanding their social circle and activities, like attending clubs and so on?

- *TWT stage three*
  Pursue the newly formed Rota Group by incorporating other benefits, like shared learning schemes after school hours, child minding support on occasional weekends.

Now it is no longer just another 'little rota project'. It's the best darn rota scheme you've ever devised! Use the means at your disposal to tackle schedules, emergency covers, snacks in the car for the kids, alternative routes to homes, CDs to play– the list is endless.

Modestly linked, reinvention process work isn't about participating in a contest to see who is the most sensible person in your neighbourhood. Often the most logical answer is probably not the best. Unless you push yourself out of a box, you'll always be squeezed into a space which is only as wide as your limited expectations of what could possibly be achieved.

A great reinvention project lets you set a task – think about what you have to accomplish, go for it, and ultimately look back on your achievement with satisfaction.

What about the second example given earlier – the customer assessment sheet? Well you could take the easy way out, fire-up your Word program on the PC, look up a template for an assessment sheet, fill in the gaps and, hey presto, the work is done. But that's as unchallenging as weight training with a feather pillow.

Be brave enough to reinvent the norm. Stretch yourself so that people buy your abilities, rather than lacklustre mediocrity. Better still, when it becomes apparent that you are a source of innovation, people around you will 'catch' the reinvention bug and start becoming more innovative for themselves. In business, this is good for you, great for your company but bad news for the competition.

How about consulting existing customers? What would they like included in the document? Speak to your boss, the team, in truth everyone associated with the business of assessment sheets. I can assure you that, at the very least, your initiative will be noted and you could get to work on a bigger and more important project. That could lead to promotion – and so your career progression moves upwards and offers fresh opportunities which, if left to fall to the ground, in the end get overlooked and under-exploited.

## The business of *you*

I try to keep the business of reinvention realistic. Believe me, it *is* a business. Just like any other business, it has to be taken seriously.

## Reinvention concerns the business of *you*: You Inc., You Plc, You.com.

Your associated customers and suppliers are those who deal with you, namely, friends, family, work colleagues and so on. Your biggest customer however is the *you* within you – the bit that sometimes nags at you in the morning and says, 'Today I feel as sluggish as my mouth before brushing my teeth.' Or beams with pride when you just know that you handled a particular assignment well. It's vital to keep *you* happy, challenged and alert.

More often than not, you don't get an instant feedback from bosses – even if you perform well. Perhaps your boss is preoccupied in a personal struggle with the Puppet Masters in HQ or takes for granted your achievements. Rather than dwell on how to react, consider instead how to respond.

In my own reinvention experience, seven out of ten bosses never bother to acknowledge gainful efforts. Perhaps they take umbrage to my style. Or have too many other things on their plate. That's all okay. Out of the remaining three who do say 'thanks', one will be ready to discuss my approach and exchange ideas; another may welcome my initiative – which is great; and the third may keep me in mind when it comes to further developing a different project – which is even better. At least, without being naïve about these things, I have something to look forward to. Who knows, over time I may even be in the position to offer input and so exert influence on what starts off as just another small project.

Best of all, providing that I approach the project to the best of my ability, using TWT:

◆ I consider what has led to a situation and project what I would prefer to happen.

◆ Closely re-examine the facts, sorting them into a series of possibilities, without being drowned by facts.

◆ Finally use sheer innovation rather than just common sense alone to arrive at a reinvention-driven answer.

Not everyone may sing and dance over my practical efforts but at least I'll be recognized – covertly, overtly or grudgingly – for being true and honest to myself and the reinvention task in hand. Try TWT in your own reinvention project.

## Pocket your own reinvention machine

Another creative reinvention thinking technique to exploit is the 'pocket reinventor'. Imagine a machine resembling a photocopier. It features four buttons:

- Enlarge

- Reduce

- Erase

- Swap

Through it you can feed an issue calling for reinvention. If you press 'enlarge' the machine shows what happens if you allowed the issue to swell. Press 'reduce' and the issue shrinks. Press 'erase' and it totally disappears. Finally, press 'swap' and you can see the effects of applying 'upside down thinking'.

So, let's say you are worried about a work colleague who always pesters you with projects that don't require your attention.

- Press 'enlarge' and you would welcome your colleague's projects to such an extent that you become overwhelmed. How would you cope? What would be your tactics?

- Press 'reduce' and the projects slow to a grinding halt. That leaves you with more time to get on with your own work. Would you honestly use that time wisely?

- Press 'erase' and the problem disappears. But so does your colleague.

- Press 'swap' and you hand some of your own projects over to your colleague.

As with all aspects of reinvention, you decide which 'buttons' to press. Your 'pocket reinventor' projects potential achievements . Use it wisely.

## Feeling good? I knew that you would

Achievement is just one set of feelings that you can draw upon to make you feel good. It's part of a psychological set of rewards which all of us seek at some point or another. Psychological rewards include praise, love, a sense of a job well done, and so on.

Yet in order to support your plans for reinvention, there are many other rewards, some elementary – yet essential to your overall well-being – which can also be tapped into. *Spirituality*, for example, brings peace of mind and a sense of high moral fibre. You can also find comfort in a *physical* approach, from keeping fit, eating the right food, pursing a healthy sex life and so on. You may also look to gain *social* rewards, these help you feel part of a community, not just in name but in deed.

Whatever set of incentives you choose as a motivational tool, the degree of anticipated rewards that you'll receive depends on your long-term commitment. Today, we all want to grasp rewards as quickly as possible. The quick sale, the quick meeting, the quick high. It's a bit like reading a self-help book. You skip the chapters and get to the ten-point, conclusion for a better life – listed at the end of the book. Sure, you may be familiar with the list, but it doesn't mean you'll understand it.

As the social and political world moves faster, so we become conditioned to expect immediate results. When a virus spreads throughout the Internet we want our emails back on-line immediately. When people diet, they want to look like a model just by taking a slimming pill rather than going on a two-mile jog. When a child is rescued from a burning building on the other side of the world, we are no longer content with TV pictures of her safe return, we expect the news teams to place a camera strapped to a fire-fighter's helmet.

## Less is more

Working on small projects helps bring you back to earth – however, not on a collision course. The smaller, more modest the project, the better. Why? If you have less to work with, you have less to lose and more to gain. But if you have vast resources to play with, though wonderful to have, you'll have to repay shareholders, colleagues, employees and so forth, their debt of support or finance.

Each will expect some kind of compensation. Which is why, if you reach a point where you have nothing or little to play with and new opportunities are rare, you are forced to step into uncomfortable reinvention zones which compel you to become more resourceful and shrewder in putting a project together.

If you are honest with yourself, you'll probably find that most of the key turning points in your life have stemmed from an uncomfortable or difficult situation. You may have fallen out of love, become bankrupt, been bullied or, worst of all, found yourself stuck in a pothole made the same time last year but once again stumbled into. Providing that you stop wallowing over your quandary and start actually doing something positive to reinvent a dilemma, such examples of adversity could provide your most outstanding instances of triumph.

## The good old, bad old days

The hardest thing in the world is not to start doing something new, but to let go of something old. Often people cling to the familiar simply because it is there or because they yearn for a distant moment in their memories when everything seemed perfect. The trouble with this is that through clinging on, any attempt at building something new is always judged against the thing which you refuse to let go. In this way, the reinvention process becomes a reprocessing procedure – grinding out near perfect facsimiles of the safely familiar. Picasso, the renowned artist, used to erase any part of a painting to which he became too attached. In this way, he forced himself to push forward boundaries rather than settle for cosiness zones.

## The trouble with living in the past is that there's no future in it.

Deal with what is in hand. Reintroduce yourself to where you stand. Reacquaint yourself with the territory as if you'd never been there before. Slowly you'll regain confidence, make friends, check out possibilities – stretch budgets – relish being in what used to appear as a discomfort zone, sealing for good the potholes and celebrating your mastery over insecurity.

### Bordering on the insane

This kind of approach also works for those seemingly boring, mundane and tedious projects at work that most people wouldn't want to touch with a barge pole! For example, some time ago I was asked to look at a project for a recruitment agency. It was a simple project: design a border around a recruitment advertisement in the local newspaper.

The border had to be in black and white. It couldn't be too fussy otherwise there would be printing problems. I spent ages examining other recruitment ads. Studying their borders, I became 'king of borders'. People thought I was nuts, I knew I was focused.

At the end of my research, I presented the most promising designs. The client was so impressed with such close attention to detail that within a week I was assigned a much bigger, more profitable task: write the advertising copy for the ads, followed by a brochure, radio commercial, campaign …

Of course, not all small projects lead to great contracts. But that's also a win-win scenario. Nothing can ever prepare you better for success than failure.

# Quitters never win. Winners never quit.

So, become a king or queen of every project and use the experience to draw upon when it comes to 'The Big One'.

## The smallest speck of ambition goes a long, long way

In the early days of Madonna's career, she wouldn't have had hundreds of hanger-ons at her beck and call. She was obviously forced into a discomfort zone to nurture a discreet, yet reliable group of contacts for support, advice and maybe even the right connections to move the project along.

You too can acquire that discreet, reliable group comprising friends and colleagues who admire the kind of achievements – those small, 'boring' yet considered projects – that you previously accomplished. Those connections – the wider the better – generate opportunities. Often people don't appreciate that if you help people with small projects, the results can be more widespread than at first assumed. A good factual analogy of this is a grain of sand. Breeze carries about 100 million tons of sand particles around the earth yearly. That means if you live in America, you could step on sand that flew in from the Gobi Desert in China.

It's only by taking the time and effort in small projects that you can ever hope to be rewarded with bigger ones with wider reaching implications. Why? The answer is similar to 'What came first – the chicken or the egg?' Both! You see, one doesn't work without the other! If you are going to get results from reinventing yourself, start at the beginning – here and now, and move on. Even if your project doesn't get you to where you initially planned, you may well end up in a more interesting – even if scary, yet thrilling–situation.

# Get to know the unfamiliar

A skydiver who has miscalculated a drop by 150 feet certainly becomes scared – but finds it exhilarating! Once you face fear, the issue that at first challenged you eventually ceases to be so terrifying. This is partly because your brain can only maintain for a limited time high levels of the chemicals that produce the emotion of fear.

To an extent, you can control the product of such chemicals with proprietary drugs and even stimulation through exercise. (*See* 'Fit Defence'.) Yet, many fears – leading to phobias – result from bad experiences. In many cases, the fear, such as fear of reinvention, can be overcome simply through direct confrontation.

Once you familiarize yourself with a frightening situation, such as working in a hostile office environment, you may continue to dislike it, even hate it, but you can't sustain that sense of fear indefinitely.

Think of it like this: imagine you are stranded in the middle of the Australian Outback. You haven't eaten properly in days. The only food within reach is a fat slimy bug. Do you eat it to survive or throw it away in disgust? The chances are high that given enough days of hunger, you will eventually eat it. Now at the moment of eating it, centimetres from your mouth, you face the bug's bulging eyes. Just by picking up the blighter proves that you have moved a step away from the fear of bugs. Next, as with any cause of fear, I suggest that the best thing to do is not linger over issues, but have the courage to just take a gulp, swallow your doubts and move on. If not, you could end up suffering from the worst of all families of phobias. First, autophobia, which inevitably leads to kakorrhaphiophobia, tropophobia and for the real hard cases phobophobia!

'Oh how I want to break free baby – God how I want to break free.'

Freddie Mercury

Breaking the circle of fear is like breaking out of any kind of self-imposed prison. Once you fracture the edges of fear, the only one who can ultimately stop you from smashing through the core of your terror is you. Sure, others can place obstacles in your way, such as political tripwires at work, but it is up to you either to confront them and plan around those obstacles or trip up on your facade and give in. Take up the challenge of your reinvention project or leave it to someone else to make progress.

Being in a rut is like looking up at a dark, overcast sky. Yet, if you were to take a flight, you would discover that even the darkest clouds are just smoke screens – above them the skies are a vivid blue.

Here's another story relating to fear of the unknown which may help to put reinvention issues into perspective. A builder staggered into the local hospital's accident and emergency department. He was in agony. He reported how a six-inch nail had gone right through his boot. He was so agitated that no one could even get near to examine him. The patient had to be calmed, so the duty doctor administered a general anaesthetic. The man fell asleep and the nursing staff slowly removed the boot. To everyone's surprise the nail had been driven between the gaps of his toes. In fact, it hadn't even grazed the skin! Yet, the man truly felt pain.

Similarly, often people become so petrified by the notion of reinvention that all sense and reasoning are thrown out of the window. On closer examination that fear turns out to be no more than a pin-prick. Face your fears and drive a nail through them.

**REINVENTING YOU**

◆ Whilst success brings good fortune, notoriety tends to conjure up curses.

◆ Success is being able to look at yourself in the mirror with confidence and a clear conscience.

▶

- Aim at revealing – in your own good time – layers of who you really are.

- What's the point of wearing 'glad-rags' if you can't wear a smile?

- Tackle problems using your head, rather than head-on.

- Your current reinvention project is not an end in itself.

- Make little projects part of your continued reinventing apprenticeship.

- Your unrealized principles are as harmful as your unfulfilled potential.

- Don't give in to your past.

- Use the Three Way Technique (TWT).

- Stretch yourself so that others invest in your abilities rather than uniformity.

- The greater your commitment to motivate yourself, the greater the rewards.

- Having less can give you more.

- Love feeling uncomfortable.

- Failure is the nursery of success.

- Become familiar with the unfamiliar.

- Beyond the clouds lies an endless vista of blue-sky potential.

reinvent yourself

moment um

04

# chapter four
## perceptions and misconceptions

Understandably, many people mistake the pursuit of reinvention for the need to change their image. To a degree, as with Madonna, they are right. However, as with Madonna, the business of focused, extensive and enduring reinvention explores makeovers in a much deeper way than just changing clothes. In doing so, it brings about a greater, more satisfactory result.

Yet, don't underestimate the role that changing image, including your choice of fashion, can play as part of your total reinvention process. As any shopper can testify, changing your wardrobe is the easiest route to feeling that you are actively participating in the whole business of reinvention. Apart from being fun and a means of escape, for a while at least, from everyday routine, it offers a quick reinvention 'fix'. Better still, if having returned home, you don't quite like the look of your new clothes, you can always go back to the shop and change them. The trouble with this of course, is that whilst the image in the mirror would have changed, the person inside the clothes will still be the same.

Matching your clothes, hairstyle, make-up and so on to reflect how you feel, and more importantly, how you want *others* to feel about you, provides in-roads to further exploring how you *act* rather than just appear.

Getting your choice of colours and style balanced is as important in business as it is in your personal life. For example, whether you like it or not, people tend to judge others on first impressions. So if you were applying for a job as a PA in a big corporate organization, turning up for the interview in a smart suit will, in most instances, probably do you more favours than turning up wearing torn jeans and builder's boots (however *à la mode* they may or may not be). On the other hand, turning up for the interview well groomed and wearing an elegant suit won't count for much if the prospective employer can't grasp the smartness of your thinking or personality, as well as clothes.

## Reinvention goes beyond shades of colours and cuts of suits.

Think about the last major conference or trade show or even club you attended. What struck you most about the people who left the most profound impression on you? Did you judge them by the colour of their outfit or the strength of their personality?

Equally, when a toddler plays with friends in a kindergarten, does he or she gravitate towards the kids who are black, white, Hispanic, Asian … or just those who seem the most fun?

Clearly, when it comes to understanding people, rather than just their projected image, the best reinventors are the ones whose vision is actually *enhanced* by colour blindness.

## Cutting to the chase

Even for people who groom images for their business, when it comes down to what's really important, circumstance rather than image can change perceptions into truth. Take the celebrity hairdresser Daniel Field. At the time of an interview with a British newspaper he was aged 42. He explained that he was brought up in a middle-class, wealthy, but not profligately rich family. His father was chairman of a public company that went bankrupt. So when it came to money matters, Daniel used to feel particularly insecure. He worked virtually non-stop every day, often cutting people's hair past midnight. After three months of maintaining such a frenetic pace, he was rushed to hospital suffering from exhaustion.

Following the death of his young nephew from leukaemia, he came to realize that all he was achieving was getting richer whilst his nephew, coincidentally aged the same as his son, was dead. 'It is not money that buys freedom, it is your attitude.'

## Flying the corporate colours

Just as your clothes reflect your style, so too companies undergoing reinvention make use of imagery to signal their meaning to the outside world as well as to their 'internal systems'. The most obvious example of such symbolism is the company logo and the colours used within that logo.

## Vivid colours alert.

## Pastel colours pacify.

## Contrasting shades stimulate.

Traditionally, the more 'professional' the company, the more non-partisan their corporate colours. During the 1990s, businesses heavily featured grey or steel colours. Today, companies reinventing their image for a more fully rounded audience tend to opt for either vivacious colours like blue on yellow or more pastel backgrounds, reflecting a gentler yet quietly confident image.

I recently was asked to analyze colours featured in company logos and then monitor what those colours were meant to represent.

I wonder how many of those companies' employees allowed their personal image of working for such organizations to be coloured by the shape and styling of the logo?

| Typical colour | Type of product/service |
| --- | --- |
| Light blue | Confident, cool, sincere and fresh/creative, solution provider. |
| Green | Fresh produce. Environmental goods, get-up-and-go products – like invigorating bath oils. (In the Middle East, green often equates to religious symbolism.) |
| Yellow | Communication, harmony, design, sales, entertainment providers. |
| Peach/Pink/Apricot | Community or sensual. |
| Purple/Maroon | Fast food, Internet, gaming, investments. |
| Red | Active, such as sporting, discos, clubs. |
| Royal or Dark blue | Educational, executive professions. |
| Mauve/ Dark red | Religious, welfare. |
| Brown | Essential, highly practical business services. |
| Gold | Higher market financial services. |
| Silver | Personal, tailor-made services. |
| Pale grey/ White | One-off services or discreet products. |
| Black | 'No nonsense' services' – e.g. legal. |

## Grab the image or get a life?

Whenever I pass a newsagent featuring the latest copy of my favourite magazines, *T3* or *Stuff*, I hang my head in shame. These magazines, and similar ones, feature glossy pages of the latest GPRS mobile phones and PDAs as well as PCs, digital music players, recorders and even back massagers, which I feel I must have – just like any other self-respecting Y2K person!

Now, before you think, 'Uh oh, I know where Jonathan is leading to … He's going to rattle on again that being at peace with yourself is better than having a piece of the latest action'. Think again.

I admire for example what Madonna has bought with some of her fortune – estimated to be worth between £200 and £400 million – such as a lavish mansion retreat. Yet, whilst I love what money buys,

I am totally besotted with the things that it can't. But successful reinvention can.

Money can buy you a clever PDA to store addresses of people whom you have met, but it can't buy their genuine friendship. Money can buy a wonderful holiday to the Tropics but it can't buy a partner to share a barefoot walk on the beach. Money can buy a four-poster bed, but it can't buy a peaceful sleep. Money can buy a leather-bound diary, but it can't buy tender memories.

**Whilst you may love what money can buy – become besotted with what it can't.**

Going back to my love for gadgets; such trinkets advertised in various magazines make me feel in touch with street life beyond my semi-detached existence in the twenty-first century. However, often I discover that once I have purchased a particular gadget, generally speaking nothing really changes– apart from having less in the bank and my general feeling of guilt about putting more on the credit card! (Does this sound familiar?)

## Designing dreams

I used to work for what must be one the trendiest technology design and marketing agencies in the UK. (For obvious reasons, I am not divulging their trading name.) Quite appropriately, as designers they had very plush offices. Their boardroom was a shrine to design. In addition to a tailor-made glass and aluminium boardroom table, there was a wall-mounted flat screen television and simple, yet elegant cabinet housing samples of classical design icons such as a Phillipe Starck lemon juicer and Nelson Atom Clock.

When it came to self-image, the agency practised what they sold to companies. For them it seemed that image was everything. The directors of the company spent as much time as possible toning up physiques. Company cars were in the class of Aston Martins. Even motorbikes had to have Ducati pedigrees. Men who worked for the agency would sneer at colleagues who didn't wear the latest Boss suits or carry inside their Porsche design briefcases, the most up-to-date Internet-connected devices. Once I asked one of the directors why the agency went to such lengths to make such striking impressions. He replied:

I am convinced that to do a job with certainty you have to feel confident in yourself. You might think it's indulgent for our account managers to drive BMWs, Jags and the like or wear Boss and Armani suits. However, when they attend a meeting, they step out of their car unruffled. Walk in on time and look a million dollars – ready to help clients make a million more.

It was all very rousing stuff. For the younger members of staff – most of whom looked like they had stepped out of the centre-pages of *Wallpaper* magazine or *GQ* and *Marie Claire* – the late nights at work and occasional champagne breakfast weekend treats were rocket-fuel for aspiring career goals.

However, despite the seductively addictive company way of life, I often wondered how the company executives felt at the end of each month having perhaps spent half of their salaries in maintaining their image rather than investing in savings accounts.

How the staff viewed life, and assessed the need for individual reinvention, was dominated by their perception of issues. For many those perceptions vary according to the gains and losses in a given situation.

Some believe that looks alone drive perceptions and that unless they are like those guys and gals who appeared to have stepped out of a trendy fashion magazine, their potential will be measured by the length of their latest haircut. (Maybe they should have a chat with Daniel.)

Of course, if that were the case, ordinary people with talent and tenacity would never have been able to achieve extraordinary things. Such people, like Richard Branson, Bill Gates and the late Larry

Adler, as indeed thousands of others from just about every walk of life, recognize that real beauty is allowing themselves to blossom.

Many of the staff at the design agency could easily have succumbed to subscribing subjective values to the sensations that encircled them. It's natural – all of us do it. (To clarify issues, I define sensations as what you see, hear and touch. Perceptions interpret those sensations, thereby giving them meaning.)

## The meaning of belief

A practical example of perceived loss or gain from a given situation would be a manager who asks a junior to make a cup of coffee. To the manager, this insignificant act may show that the team member is also a team player. Whereas to the team member, just the image of making coffee may be perceived to be just another chore for the 'run-around'.

It is often claimed that for every two engaged in a debate, there are two thousand points of view! Perhaps. What is certain is that whilst you can never choose your family, you can choose the meaning and significance that you attach to any situation. Like any event in history, the facts surrounding a given situation remain fixed. Whilst the way in which you deal with a set of circumstances are as focused, broad or sweeping as your perspective.

## Is it you or your beliefs?

Meanings give rise to beliefs, which in turn conjure up images – if you like, *projections* – of what the future may hold and what your role will be in that prospect. Beliefs (not necessarily those including religious philosophies) are an integral part of life. When you take a fresh look at your beliefs, you'll find that they reflect everything about your life.

**Reinvent your beliefs about what makes you happy in life, and you'll change your world.**

If you are unable to quit smoking, many assume it is due to a lack of will power. If you put on weight from not exercising, many will say you have not taken care of yourself. If you can't find a boyfriend or girlfriend, you may conclude that you are unlovable (depending on the availability of eligible partners). All these beliefs are only there because people choose, and so imagine them to be. Equally, for many, beliefs are followed, not so much because of what they choose to envisage but because of what they choose *not* to see.

## Image in a class of its own

The devastating attack on the World Trade Center in New York and the Pentagon in Washington on 11 September 2001, which killed thousands of innocent people, unleashed a reinvented form of warfare that no military analyst had ever imagined possible. Among other casualties were major airlines and travel companies which suddenly found themselves deprived of hordes of transatlantic route passengers who had developed an acute fear of flying. Invariably, drastic staff layoffs followed.

Despite saving operational costs through redundancies, airlines still had to fly to make a living. Their most lucrative source of income had always come from business class passengers. More than ever, the airlines felt compelled to keep their 'best customers' satisfied.

With this in mind, I was asked to participate in some business-class flyers research, not as a customer, but an observer. A group of 25 business class flyers were invited into a specially adapted hospitality lounge in London. A trained facilitator asked questions about their attitudes towards flying.

Along with the other observers I watch the proceedings from behind a one-way mirror.

'Are you afraid of flying?'

*'Not at all.'*

'Have the adverse reports in the media made you think twice about flying again?'

'No.'

'How do you think recent terror events affect airlines, and in particular their relationship with business class passengers?' The group thought about this question, then one answered:

*'The airlines will have to improve their service.'*

'Do you mean, improve security?'

*'Well'*, interjected one passenger, *'I suppose they could reinforce the partition which divides business class from economy. Also, when someone in economy becomes too rowdy, maybe they could throw a net over him, so keeping him quiet until the plane landed safely.'*

Astonishingly, on the whole, no one had any particularly strong views on issues about terrorist security. Instead, the main conclusions were:

◆ Improve the choice of in-flight entertainment.

◆ Ask the stewards and stewardesses to smile more often.

◆ Include amongst the crew a muscular steward (suggested by one of the female passengers).

◆ Rather than a full meal, offer passengers the option to have a hamburger and glass of chardonnay wine.

◆ (Above all) *We are business people; it will take much more than politics to stop us getting on with the business of simply doing business.*

All of which proved to everyone observing from behind the one-way mirror that to change perceptions, you need to be concerned with much more than an image presented in the media – whether of composure or horror. Instead, seek to understand people's core values and motives from their perspective. Only then can you begin to encourage them to reinvent their perceived image of themselves.

## Addressing perceptions

Many management consultancy firms are paid fortunes to resolve complex problems surrounding the issue of how companies see themselves against how their customers view them. To address this, they sort the problems of perception into flow charts resembling family trees. At the root of the problem are all the issues that most obviously need to be addressed.

These are separated by issues that can be categorized into distinctive sections or branches. Anything that can't be addressed under each issue is given its own branch of the 'tree'. This in turn has its own family of leaves representing the effects of any branch issue. Although directly connected to the branch, the leaves are of course also part of the overall structure.

Once all the issues have been sketched out, a consultancy firm can see at a glance where the root cause of the problem lies. The leaves represent the effects of the issues, which have been generated by the problems. Then, with the mapped out tree in hand, it is just a matter of advising on possible steps to resolve each issue. Such advice is then put to the test by seeing how in practice rather than theory, each resolution either improves or worsens a situation.

Upon seeing the surface manifestation of a problem – its 'leaf' – many people become convinced that in order to resolve specific issues, all that is required is to treat that particular 'leaf'. In some cases, directly dealing with the 'leaf' will put an end to the matter. However, in many other cases the leaf is only a small part of a greater problem.

## Just what the doctor ordered

It's like going to the doctor complaining of a rash. You tell the doctor that the rash appeared a week ago after touching a stinging nettle. The doctor – rather like a management consultant – listens to your symptoms and diagnosis and then, taking an independent approach, suggests how the problem fits into the bigger scheme of things.

Sometimes when dealing with your own reinvention ambitions, it's worthwhile thinking of yourself as a doctor, taking a broader, yet considered view of issues. The question as to whether you can just as easily take the prescribed medicine to cure the problem is of course a different issue altogether!

## When it comes to giving and taking advice, be prepared to take your own medicines.

### Six billion heads are better than one

One other technique to resolve the difference between perception and reality is to put yourself in the shoes of those able to shed light on the issue.

For example, let's say you are having problems with a boss who keeps on piling up the work, whilst you are trying to beat the clock. However quickly (and efficiently) you manage to plough through the projects, the boss still manages to top up the in-tray on your desk which begins to look like the ground-base for Mount Everest.

Throughout this book I have urged you not to copy others, but take the lead for yourself. That doesn't mean though that you can't profit from your admiration of others.

Imagine you want to throw a dinner party and could invite anyone in the world as your guests. (Over six billion people to choose from!) At your table you find yourself surrounded by famous personalities whom you have long admired. Now ask each how they would deal with the problem of your boss and the mountainous stack of work and jot down their expert advice. Of course, in reality those ideas would be from your own fertile imagination. Which means your perception of how others, whom you regard as better qualified than yourself, would tackle the problem will help resolve it. Best of all, the knowledge that in reality that resolution was of your own making will strengthen your confidence.

# Let's talk about *you*

It all boils down to self-esteem. Many people mistakenly believe that self-esteem concerns vain boastfulness. It doesn't. Just as you have the natural ability to act on instincts, you have natural talents. Maybe you are a great manager or have an artistic streak running through you …

Your talents combined with how you implement and reinvent them are unique to you. Celebrate them! Once you are happy with yourself, you can begin to feel more comfortable with everyone around you. And guess what – they'll feel happy about dealing with you too!

Whatever the degree of your own image, although ostensibly it mirrors to the outside world who you are supposed to be, in your mind's eye it presents who you are really. So whether into Boss suits, Oxfam blouses, Palm Pilot PDAs, Phillipe Starck lemon squeezers, or second-hand Ford cars, your image is your own choice.

You won't drop down dead if you don't have the latest props when stepping out into the world to feel unruffled and confident within yourself. The only actuality is your perception. Only you can decide which perception to choose. I hope that given the chance to understand how you arrive at that choice, you'll have the self-esteem to wear your image with confidence and pride.

In conclusion, when it comes to perceptions and misconceptions, often people arrive at the need to reinvent themselves because they have stumbled in one form or another and in doing so have fallen into a self-fulfilling belief of what will happen to them next. I think that in terms of keeping things in perspective, stumbling can be a blessing! When you stand upright and walk ahead, you see life from an eye-level view. Yet once you stumble, you notice the small details – at ground level – which support the bigger issues. Recognizing these finer details helps you gain an even greater appreciation of what direction to take and so deepens your perspective on issues calling for you to stand up and march forward.

◆ You are a person, not a label.

◆ Wear reinvention on your sleeve but live it in your heart.

◆ Makeovers are more substantial than changing your clothes.

◆ Is your thinking as sharp as your suits?

◆ Reinvention goes beyond shades of colours and cuts of suits.

◆ Whilst you may love what money can buy – become besotted with what it can't.

◆ Real beauty is allowing yourself to blossom.

◆ Whilst you can never choose your family, you can choose the meaning and significance that you attach to any situation.

◆ Reinvent your beliefs about what makes you happy and you'll change your world.

◆ Seek to understand people's core values and motives and you'll encourage them to reinvent how they see themselves.

◆ Map out your perceptions and then deal with them, from the root upwards.

◆ When it comes to giving and taking advice, be prepared to take your own medicine.

◆ Turn your perceptions about how others would resolve issues, into practical ways to resolve them for yourself.

chapter four

# chapter five

## don't dream of a revolution: realize your own evolution

Three situations I detest: serious illness, funerals and certain types of board meetings, when people pick over the flesh of a dead project in a bogus, ulterior motive-driven attempt at reinventing what clearly should be laid to rest. What do these situations have in common? People acting when it's too late.

I hate the apparent unfairness of a seriously debilitating disease like cancer, renal failure or heart disease. All these maladies and more often bring sufferers to a full realization of what should be most highly valued in life – good health, loving families and genuine friends as well as, of course, contentment. Instead, most of us waste too much time trying to hold on tightly to good intentions, which are as ephemeral and fragile as butterflies, and just as difficult to keep alive.

In my experience, upon learning of a relative's imminent demise, previously ostracized sons, daughters, brothers and sisters pluck up their courage and seek confession by the death-bed. On such occasions, pent-up unspoken truths truss the visitors in an invisible straitjacket of guilt and remorse.

Regardless of the 'if only's', the kindest act that is often expressed in a family setback is a simple smile, a sincere look of love and a compassionate hug. Some people call it 'getting back to basics'. I like to think of it as getting back to the things that really matter, whether in business or at home.

**You needn't wait until your last breath to get back to basics.**

# Take courage to face reality

As to certain board meetings, I can't stomach the 'well, I knew it would never work' attitude of various vultures preening their feathers in eagerness of the anticipated blood-fest. Or the red tape involved in updating an employee's job description form. Often, rather than helping an employee reinvent their prospects, such plutocratic-driven exercises serve first to remind the employee of their luck and the employee's benevolence that they have a job in the first place – never mind any pseudo prospects for a pay rise. Second, they provide the manager with an excuse to off-load excess work on to someone else's shoulders. Third, they reaffirm the manager's ruling position over his or her department's workforce.

It's the sense of duplicity that I detest in these people who rarely show the courage to support a project – through facing challenges and dealing with them during the good and bad times. Hapless managers remain tongue-tied as they face the stares of inquisitors. (Their thoughts fixed on how to make the next mortgage repayment rather than addressing the corporate reinvention projects at hand.)

It never fails to amaze how much extra effort is invested in endeavours when only a limited time is left. (Rather like the common practice of putting off revising for an exam until the night before.) It's as if we have been avoiding what needed to be done – what needed to be faced – for as long as practical until cornered into taking some kind of action. Depending on the scope which is open to us, measured by how much time we have left, we either act willingly or reluctantly – allowing for space to wriggle out of the predicament.

It's a lot easier to start your own evolution now, rather than waiting for something dramatic to happen soon, in order to cause a revolution. Do so and you'll never have to say 'it's too late'.

# The green-eyed face of reinvention

As a child I watched the television series, *The Incredible Hulk*. In it the lead character, Dr David Banner, takes part in an experiment that goes horribly wrong. An overdose of so-called 'Gamma Rays' alters his DNA whenever he gets angry. So much so that he physically changes into a raging, muscle-bound, green-fleshed monster – The Incredible Hulk.

The monster is a misconstrued creature who tries, albeit clumsily, to improve situations for people facing adversity. However, in his gauche attempt to improve matters, the green, ugly and lumbering, Incredible Hulk tends to destroy just about everything in his path. Just as The Hulk only manifests itself when Dr Banner is angry, so too when he calms down, his DNA reverts to his normal 'human form'.

Throughout the series, Dr Banner seeks a cure for his condition and endures the consequences of his rampaging, in the knowledge that if his alter-ego were ever discovered, he would surely pay the ultimate price. At the beginning of each programme, Dr Banner gazes down at his own grave – which in fact contains no corpse yet. This is a necessary facade to protect his true identity.

As a child watching that programme wondering what my own future held in store, I can assure you that it was all very moving stuff. One of the lessons I learnt from Banner is that when I get annoyed, even flustered at others, perhaps the real cause of my anger is not just them but my muddled up way of dealing with the situation in which they have landed me. If I can change my approach perhaps I will also change the conclusion, rather than have a green-eyed angry view of myself and those around me.

## Write your own obituary

Imagine that you too were a Dr Banner figure grieving over the death of your past. Picture reading your own epitaph. What would those 30 odd words say about you? Were you a good, kind person? Would you be missed by relatives and friends? Were you a person about whom people spoke highly? A reliable colleague or just another would-be contender in a contentious world?

As an integral part of many of my marketing lectures, students are asked to recount the history of their lives in just 60 words.

For me, the most intriguing aspect of the exercise is what people choose to leave out.

Time and again, when personal histories are recounted, entire childhoods are skipped or family relationships passed over. The question I explore is whether those omissions occur because of their apparent insignificance to the students' lives or whether they are in fact so overwhelmingly significant that they are just too painful to recall and so confront.

You may find that confronting a personal reinvention issue is more difficult in practice than theory. To achieve ideal results you need to lose any previous negative mindset you've picked up along the way. The problem is, many of us try a direct route by heading straight to whatever helps you cope best in life, even if that coping mechanism doesn't make any sense either logically or health-wise.

For example, several times I have tried to lose weight. I appreciate why I should lose weight and know what to do. Yet thinking about it tends to drive me to the nearest chocolate shop to buy a couple of bars, which paradoxically help sweeten my conscience. The same applies for drinking, gambling or any other habit we want to rid ourselves of – including bad behavioural or thinking habits themselves.

## I would if I could but I won't

Many of us are full of good intentions and unfulfilled actions. It's like being at a sales meeting, promising to meet targets, but falling short simply because you sold the hype and even bought into it yourself, rather than core product values.

It's also rather like being arrested for drink driving. 'I intended not to drink and drive, M'Lud', you plead to the judge. (Try telling that to the road accident victim.) Or suffering a heart attack through over-exertion. 'I intended to slow down', you reason, rather pathetically with the doctor. Whatever your intentions, and circumstances, remember this old maxim:

# If you always do what you always did, you'll always get what you always got!

Whatever the age, many of us do illogical things for simple reasons. Our actions make us feel better – albeit temporarily. When the guilt sets in (which it does invariably) the only cure is the more direct one – a beeline to do it all over again!

Many find it hard to reinvent set lives because they simply cannot break habits offering 'quick-fix' comforts. That's natural. I can certainly be counted among those addicted to doing wrong things which help make me feel better about my wrongdoings!

Perhaps the best way to break the cycle is to look at what is actually being achieved. If you look for something that helps you feel better, you need first to recognize and accept that it will only provide a quick-fix rather than a sustained, satisfactory solution. Then, and only then, can you begin to separate the cause and effect of your actions.

If you can find another way to get a similar, even better result, without causing any harm, you should give it a go. That calls for commitment, courage and tenacity. Once you get on with changing your set life and the habits provisionally supporting or alleviating your concerns, then you can move on to improve other areas.

This is harder than it sounds. Habits protecting our soft-centred vulnerabilities are tough to crack. Yet, once you recognize that *what you get* – that sense of fulfilment spawned by the habit – is driven by *what you give*, your behavioural pattern can begin to progress at a good pace.

I knew a lawyer who worked in-house for an oil company. Many of his acquaintances believed that in addition to being highly competent, he was also highly confident. Yet, he confided in me that, deep down, he felt anything but self-assured. Whilst he knew how to defend others, when it came to his own position, he would be the first to convict himself of any accusation.

It is hardly surprising therefore that he never made it to head of department material. Instead, he allowed himself to be bullied by various, more assertive people, who were given the department's top slot. The lawyer used the bullying tactics to justify to himself why he needed to work so hard at winning cases, and the bosses just exploited him to further their own self-centred careers not just at the practice but with future employers in mind, who would want managers with a good track record of 'getting the most' from their team. To this date, the lawyer remains at the firm. He still feels bitter over his inability to defend his own rights.

## Find the root cause of your problems and pull it out

Old habits stop people from growing wise. The easiest, most direct paths to fulfilment often misdirect people who refuse to move on, especially in the workplace. Their habits are like garden weeds. If you leave a stretch of lawn to wilt in the sun it will first turn yellow-green, and then to hay. However, weeds, like habits, have very deep roots and so they flourish – even in the midday sun. To destroy them you have to dig deep to find their root cause and pull them out. If you persist in indulging in an activity which ultimately only provides a quick-fix distraction away from what is really bothering you, you end up deluding yourself that 'everything is okay'. In reality you are just clinging on to familiar security blankets (always an easier option than exploring the extent of your hitherto hidden talent to find a better, ultimately more satisfying way to reinterpret and so reinvent a set of circumstances from the roots upwards).

## Tools of the trade

Within yourself you possess all the emotional tools to fix counter-productive behaviour. They include:

◆ experience

◆ values

◆ potential

◆ courage

◆ intuition

◆ determination

◆ talents

◆ passion

As well as

◆ Your ...

◆ Your...

◆ Your...

◆ Your...

(I shall leave the last four blank for you to complete.)

## Don't look back in anger

Psychologists and even motivational 'gurus' often discuss a condition called 'Perceptual Defence'. This happens when, as a self-defensive measure against having to face an important issue head-on

– like a difficult boss at work, or an uncooperative partner – the mind prevents you from accepting  the reality of a situation.

Commonly, this may be a parent who 'doesn't see' that their beloved child has a drug problem rather than a homework crisis. Or a spouse who refuses to accept that their partner has fallen out of love; or worse still that they themselves have fallen out of love.

Whilst not everything that is faced can be changed, invariably, little can ever change until you face up to it. Once a psychologist can show the patient how to recognize habitual patterns of conflict, conditions invariably begin to improve.

## Recognize reality – then move on.

You can do the same by looking back at difficult periods in your life. Jot down the typical patterns that ultimately led you to make a bad decision; even when initially it may have seemed a promising path. Those patterns may not have been entirely of your own making, but at least by seeing – literally on paper – which parts were of your design, you can avoid the same mistakes in the future.

## Four faces of anger

Anger is a common reaction when faced with a situation in which you feel you have lost control. Anger manifests itself in four key ways:

◆ *Purposeful anger*
This is intentional with a significant degree of consideration or calculation as well as a considerable amount of self-control.

◆ *Spontaneous anger*
This kind of anger sparks off at the slightest thing. It isn't planned and offers little, if any, self-control.

◆ *Constructive anger*
This type of anger affirms and acknowledges a person's integrity

and social boundaries without straying too far into other people's social boundaries or compromising their integrity.

♦ *Defensive anger*
  When people feel cornered, they may turn to defensive anger. It fortifies their vulnerability through intent to violate another person's integrity and social boundary – irrespective of whether that intention is conscious or not.

So next time you fall into a downwards spiralling path towards greater and greater anger, take the time at least to discover what kind of anger you are experiencing. Then maybe, rather than feeding that anger with negativity, you could turn it into a powerful force for re-thinking your approach towards a situation. Who knows? You could even end up reinventing what would otherwise have been another episode of unconstructive thoughts, leading to disruptive actions and general unhappiness.

## Needs and fears

The people you meet have needs and fears just like you. Getting the most from those people– and finding a better way to improve personal circumstances through reinvention – means collaborating and discovering techniques that deliver what others want, whilst also achieving what you need and deserve.

There are a number of joint requirements which can be utilized to attain common goals. First, there is the need to implement a personal agenda, rather than fulfil a communal commitment. In other words, people tend to co-operate with others in order to fulfil their own ambitions. If their agenda supports yours – all the better.

People gravitate to people who share similar ideologies and pleasures. At the very least, people are attracted to those who give the impression of being kindred spirits. Of equal importance is the attraction exerted by those who strive to do their best not simply to impress others but because they genuinely enjoy what they do. It shows character. Once you connect with people, more often than not, you will begin to enjoy the greatest of all interpersonal rewards – trust.

People tend to listen and grasp only the issues with which they can personally identify. So, irrespective of the amount of effort that went into delivering that content, any great idea will never materialize unless it can be communicated in an effective manner that speaks directly to the people whom you are trying to influence. If that calls for simple language or practical examples that highlight key points, then you have to deliver.

## The best bits are invariably between the covers

For example, I took my 10-year-old son Joshua to the Natural History Museum in London. He wanted to buy a souvenir so we visited the gift shop. Whilst Joshua looked at the toy display, I flicked through the books. One in particular caught my eye, *The Prehistory of the Mind*.

I glanced at the blurb on the sleeve. It all appeared very impressive; in fact, I bought the book. However, I had no real intention to read it. My plans were far more devious: I intended to place it strategically on a prominent part of my bookshelf. This way when guests looked at my library, they would assume that I must be some kind of genius to read such intricate 'egg-head' material!

Some time later, I didn't have anything to read. My usual collection of gossip and TV soap magazines was waiting to be replenished. Then I remembered the book from the Natural History Museum. Reluctantly I opened it. Before long, to my surprise, I discovered that the content was easy and interesting to follow. You see, despite the fact that the subject matter was complex, the author managed to communicate the message in such a simple way that even a layperson like me could understand it.

So, when trying to deal with difficult people, ensure that your superficial defensive bravado isn't covering up a well-intentioned message. Rather than make matters worse through poor communication, get on a level footing. This leaves the way clear to explain your views in terms that everyone will understand, and through doing so, more people will come to appreciate. The same is true when explaining your reinvention methodology. Right from the outset, providing your rationale is sound, the easier it is to understand, the more sense it will make for everyone involved.

## Make reinvention personal

In marketing, you soon learn that the most important word in anybody's vocabulary is his or her name. For example, the more you personalize a letter or piece of direct marketing correspondence, the better the results. This guiding principle doesn't just relate to a name but where a prospect lives, working and social preferences, financial status and so on. Equally, the more you can demonstrate that what you are selling enhances personal worth in terms of esteem, wealth, aspirations, perceptions and so on, the better. In fact, if you can demonstrate that the tangible benefits of your sales proposition are more favoured towards the prospect than to you – the more receptive they'll become.

## Everyone wants to be a 'somebody'.

The more you can make people feel that they are appreciated as part of a community – albeit, working, family or social – the better.

Many managers in today's workplace supervise teams in order to protect, defend or enhance their own self-esteem. On the other hand, life's true mentors, who are sadly few and far between, aim to have their abilities outshone by those of their apprentices.

Nobody wants to feel rejected. Everybody wants to be loved – perhaps at work through some kind of recognition of achievements. If you can show how your reinvention makes others look, feel or sound 'good', then clearly 'selling' reinvention becomes much easier.

## Perception is truth

It's all a matter of perception – theirs. Which brings me to another aspect of marketing. If you can get people to believe in something that isn't actually seen – and yet appreciated as important in the mind of consumer, then you can get them to 'see' anything you like. This is core to brand communications.

It's a matter of belief and trust. Both of which add up to truth. When it comes to marketing your own reinvention to the people who count, one of your greatest weapons will always be perception. And perception, whether focused through military propaganda, advertising hype, public relations platitudes, or the lens of the camera, tends to be equated with truth.

## There's not much in view when your head is stuck in the sand

There are some key personality traits, or habits, that make reinventing yourself very difficult. And there are others that are absolutely crucial. Refusal to face up to the need for change heads the list of obstacles. Maybe you absolutely refuse to accept that there is a problem with something or someone – or with yourself. For example, you possibly are about to lose an important account at work because you simply didn't service it properly. However, you kid yourself that the cause of the problem lies with the client rather than yourself.

It reminds me of when I was a teenager on holiday in the summer that Elvis Presley died. News reached us of the King's demise. The group was very sad – all except one who foolishly cried, 'A man like Elvis is too great to be dead'. At first I thought he meant that his spirit and music would never die. But I was wrong. He literally meant that Elvis as a human being couldn't die!

People who refuse to accept and face real problems, including the fact that they could be playing an integral role in the origins of the quandary, are living in a fantasy world, fuelled by delusions rather than decisiveness.

Many of these people will buy management books advocating positive thinking. Or as I like to think of such titles –'How to stick your head in the ground whilst praying that passers-by can see the sun shining out of your backside'.

Just because you manage to smile a lot and chant 'I am a wonderful person' 557 times a day, or 'my ego is/isn't directly correlated to the size of my genitals' or 'the newly appointed Cambridge educated male Head of Department really is only stirred by the strength of my thinking, rather than the tautness of my bra-strap', it doesn't mean that life at work or at home will fundamentally change.

Positive energy comes from positive action which spawns success, which breeds positive thinking. But the cycle can never start unless you begin to face your problems head-on rather than through an occasional series of backward glances.

Positive thinking didn't make Einstein an eminent scientist and reinventor of the possible. It took hard graft. As he said, 'I think and think for months and years. Ninety-nine times the conclusion is false. The hundredth time, I am right.' Like all people committed to reinvention, Einstein stuck to the reality of change in order to become unstuck from traditional accepted wisdom.

Walt Disney was sacked by a newspaper for showing little, if any, artistic imagination on the job! Even his first cartoon production company, Laugh-O-Gram, went into liquidation. Perseverance as well as self-belief proved his critics and creditors wrong.

## Never give up

At the time of writing, the Kentucky Fried Chicken restaurant chain has over 9,900 restaurants in 82 countries across the world and serves a staggering 2 billion chicken meals a year.

But it wasn't always so 'finger lickin' good' for the company. I once heard a legendary story of how the founder, Colonel Harland Sanders, developed his secret recipe of a blend of 11 herbs and spices back in the 1930s. For years the Colonel carried his secret recipe in his head and the spice mixture in his car.

Legend has it that he eventually had the idea to sell the recipe to any restaurant which wanted it, on one proviso: that they would pay a royalty on every chicken piece ever sold thereafter. Most people laughed at the idea! In fact the Colonel was shown the door – usually the back one – time after time after time. Yet the Colonel was determined to reinvent the way chicken could be sold. In all, 1,000 times he tried until one restaurateur agreed to the deal.

## To you it's garnish, to me the parsley's the icing on the cake

Another story relates to a greengrocer called Clement Halfon. In his pursuit of reinvention, he never settled for instant rejections. For example, he wanted to secure a substantial order from a private members dining club in London. At the time, my father was executive head chef at the club in Pall Mall. Halfon asked if he could be included on the list of preferred fruit suppliers. My father, who was constantly approached by suppliers, politely said 'no'. Yet, unlike most other suppliers, Halfon persisted. Each week he would call my father extolling the virtues of his fruit and vegetables. Still my father declined.

He was widely known by suppliers as being tough, demanding the highest possible standards.

Then one week, Halfon visited my father at the club, 'Look, why don't you buy just *a bunch of parsley*?' he asked, holding a small bunch in his hand. 'I promise you that it is the finest, freshest parsley you have ever tasted.' My father was so enchanted by such an outrageous proposal that he reached into his pocket and paid the 20 pence for the bunch of parsley himself.

Before long, Halfon supplied all the fruit and vegetables for the club. Later, my father became the executive head chef of the House of Commons. Halfon naturally followed as the official supplier of all fruit and vegetables.

The story was typical. Halfon was renowned for not taking 'no' for an answer, even on one occasion when another chef in London's West End district became so flabbergasted by Halfon's persistence that he threatened him with a meat cleaver! (That chef too eventually became a lifetime customer.) In fact, Clement went on to be one of the most respected and successful greengrocers in the United Kingdom. (Who says money doesn't grow on trees?)

## Never take your reinvention for granted

Positive thinking alone doesn't get a job done. However, it gives you hope that one day a situation will improve. Once that happens there is scope for reinvention. Where there's perseverance, there is scope, which provides hope – the most powerful of all fuels – to drive your realistic ambitions, rather than shallow intentions, ahead at full speed.

Don't be one of these, though, who are in such a rush that they end up looking like asses. By this, I mean that they jump to assumptions without first carefully checking the facts. They are unwilling to question motives in depth (theirs or anyone else's). Hence, *'assume'*, makes an ASS of U and ME.

I also want to mention the apathetics. They become crucified by their own fears and refusal to accept a situation not to their liking. Then they try either to kid themselves that the problem is not there or, if it persists, that somehow fate will take care of it. Or that, having got away with a situation many times before, they will surely get away with it again – despite all evidence pointing to the contrary: Truly the mirror is a fool's most captivated audience!

Finally, there are those who stand on cliff tops, defiantly challenging the wind of change and reinvention, their mouths shrouded by chiffon scarves. In terms of protection, the scarves are of course useless other than for concealing their contorted grin of sheer terror. No one ever comes to their rescue, because no one sees their distress.

You may recognize traits of any of the above in your own psyche. Whatever your problem, until and unless you start to acknowledge its existence, you will never fully deal with it.

## Don't come out fighting: end up winning

The biggest battles in your life will be fought within yourself. Eastern philosophers observe that looking for happiness outside yourself is meaningless. It's like expecting to become fit by watching others exercise.

They are right. To be a winner it's pointless surrendering to any misguided self-deception that everything is just hunky-dory. That is not to say you should be a pessimist. Far from it: in reinventing yourself, first and foremost appreciate that only you can achieve happiness through conquering self-doubts. Let those around you remain fumbling about in the fog.

'Against every great and noble endeavour are a thousand mediocre minds.'

Albert Einstein

I truly believe that everyone is a natural born winner and becomes author of his or her own style of reinvention. Reaching the winning post is a great responsibility demanding hard graft. After all, it is easy to reach towards responsibility, but slippery to grasp. Few take it, many more prefer to pass it on.

Not fulfilling your potential actually saps your energy. Don't you find that when you do next to nothing all day long, you feel especially tired? Yet, when you are kept busy, you feel more energetic. Energize yourself – now. Don't wait. Once you get things rolling – keep on rolling. Or as the Japanese say, 'Flowing water never goes bad'.

You too may have resolved to give up drugs, drinking, gambling, binging, women – or whatever else avoids dealing with the real issues that bother you. Yet making a promise isn't the same as actually carrying it out. A wise rabbi once said, 'Say little, do a lot'.

## Don't just say what you want to happen or change, *do it.*

(Maybe the rabbi was spiritual advisor to the management board at Nike – 'Just Do It'.)

Once you are committed to making a change, think of your commitment as a morally binding contract between your mind and soul. Follow through that commitment by seeking solutions rather than making excuses. For example, you can't excuse yourself for putting on weight because you accidentally ate a double McDonald's quarter-pound cheeseburger and extra large fries, followed by two ice-creams, a bag of donuts and a packet of liquorice!

Following through a reinvention commitment will not only help you philosophically and psychologically, it will strengthen your emotional characteristics and so appeal in whatever you choose.

## Ain't no mountain high enough to keep you from you

Time, money and effort are invested in people to ensure that they carry out their responsibilities as effectively as their convictions. It's why we listen to doctors. Hope dictates that the doctor knows how to save the patient. Actions on their part, producing the right diagnosis, reaffirm our belief and faith in them. Such actions are never easy to grasp. Life is never easy: if it were, it wouldn't be so intriguing. Just because your life may have taken a wrong turn, it doesn't mean that you have ended up in a cul-de-sac.

Some describe life as 'an uphill struggle'. I suggest that you celebrate the prospect of climbing that hill. If life were just a merry downhill ride from start to finish, you would never have the time to appreciate the scenery. You'd be hurtling down too fast. You would never experience the sense of achievement as well as praise, for having overcome those hurdles.

## *You* in action: the child that realized its visions

When you plan for successful reinvention and are determined to succeed, you probably will – in one way or another. In an interview with the Chicago press, the notable TV polymath and one of the United States best-loved reinvented celebrities Oprah Winfrey, explained her childhood visions.

I was raised on a farm with my grandmother. I knew somehow that my life would be different and better. I remember gaining that feeling at the age of four.

I stood on the back porch. My grandmother was boiling clothes in a great big iron pot. She was poking them down. As I watched her, I promised that my life wouldn't be like this. It will be better. And it wasn't from a place of arrogance, it was just a place of knowing that things could somehow be different.

Leaders never achieve greatness by continually going downhill. On beginning the ascent of the mountain, they become familiar with the terrain and how to navigate it. It applies to you as well. The climb will strengthen your physical as well as emotional muscles. The more you climb – the higher you'll reach, defeating the paradox that 'the higher you climb, the further and faster you'll fall'.

When confronted with a mountain of problems, most of us tend to blame systems, governments, the economy, and anything else other than ourselves that we can cling to by our fingertips. That's natural.

**'We are in a fight for our principles, and our first responsibility is to live by them.'**

President George W. Bush

Three days after the world's worst terrorist attack, in which thousands were murdered in New York, to commemorate the victims, there was a Europe-wide three minutes' silence in commemoration of the victims. At 11 am on Friday 14 September I was driving. Along with other motorists in London I stopped the car by the side of the road, stood and thought about the atrocious event, especially what individuals could do to improve matters – however modestly. Nearby, some people sitting at a bus stop wearing Levi jeans and munching on McDonald's hamburgers, looked on in bemusement. Judging by their looks, apparently for them, another country's problems were the problems of that country. Anything 'American' had nothing to do with their lives.

As long as people refuse to take personal responsibility for making change, however great or small – even three minutes' worth of time – then in terms of reinvention, the world will never alter and the only ones who will be accountable for the subsequent cost will be ourselves.

## It's not my problem mate

Study commercial history. You will invariably discover that, irrespective of economic climates, people who take their responsibilities seriously – buying into what they believe is a *genuine* market need, demanding the resolve and application that only they and their product or service can employ – turn out to be winners in one form or another.

Some may end up becoming millionaires. Others may discover opportunities that are even more profitable perhaps spiritually or emotionally.

## Like the SAS motto, those who dare win.

Study political, social and cultural history. You will also learn that great leaders have not possessed commonly innate gifts. Instead, applying their natural talents to the best of their abilities, they responded to social and cultural trends.

|  | Strength | Weakness |
|---|---|---|
| Freud | Linguistic, personal | Spatial, musical |
| Einstein | Logical, spatial | Scholarly |
| Eliot | Linguistic, scholarly | Musical |
| Gandhi | Personal, linguistic | Artistic |

## Follow the leaders, then lead

Rather than grumble about being hampered by some external organization, reinvention winners re-examine and enhance their internal system. Richard Branson, when he first started, had so little money that he conducted much of his business from a telephone box in Tottenham Court Road, London.

Or take the boxer, Larry Holmes. One of 11 children, Holmes dropped out of seventh grade to work and support his fatherless family. Before he became a boxer, he was a truck driver and janitor. Holmes explains: 'Without a full education, you can't continue in sports such as baseball, basketball or football. You can't make it either as an athlete unless you go into a field like boxing.'

Even though many told him, 'You'll never make it, the other boxers are too good', the extra effort paid off. He lost in his attempt to make the 1972 Olympics boxing team, but continued to spar with such boxers as Mohammed Ali and Ken Norton, who were also renowned for their courage to change destinies.

Many years later Holmes was given his first big break. That challenge led to victory over third-ranked Earnie Shavers and a shot at the World Boxing Council's heavyweight crown. After 15 challenging rounds with then titleholder Ken Norton, Holmes was crowned Champ.

To reinvent themselves, even the world's greatest figures – people like Roosevelt, Churchill, Martin Luther King and Mother Theresa – fought issues like poverty, ill health and even child abuse.

On 26 January 1956, the young Martin Luther King was arrested for driving at 30 mph in a 25 mph zone. Four days later, the family home was fire-bombed. If King had not found the courage to speak up for himself and his community, he would have become just another casualty of a bigoted society.

In 1957, King became the first president of the Southern Christian Leadership Conference. King's dreams raised the hopes of the oppressed weighed down by the oppressors. He dreamt and eventually realized the impossible odds against reaching a promise of equality.

## It's time to wake up to what is happening in your life right now.

This moment is part of the threads making up the pattern of your own historical tapestry. Unless you are prepared to exploit – especially the difficult issues which your competitors won't – you may never be in a position to enjoy things which your competitors can't.

# You don't have to be a giant to walk tall.

You don't have to be incapacitated by illness before appreciating what you've got. You don't have to stand by a deathbed to say what you feel. You don't have to wait for others to endorse your sense of conviction. You don't have to mourn the loss of having too little time to turn enemies into allies or yourself into someone even greater. We all have limited numbers of heartbeats to drum out during our lifetime. Start enjoying and reaching the full potential of your life – according to *your* tempo.

## REINVENTING YOU

- Don't wait until your dying breath to make amends with yourself and others.

- You may not be able to change what people think, but you can change what you think about people.

- If you always do what you always did, you'll always get what you always got.

- Change bad habits – habitually.

- What you get depends on what you give.

- Recognize reality, then move on.

- Know the difference between purposeful, spontaneous, constructive and defensive anger.

- Everyone has common needs: address them.

- Aim to be trusted.

- People understand your thinking when it addresses theirs.

- Keep reinvention simple.

- Face up to realities rather than hiding your head in the sand.

- Positive thinking never works without positive doing.

- Perseverance generates hope which offers scope for reinvention.

- Losers look at what they are going through. Winners look *where* they are going to.

- The greatest battles are often fought out in your mind.

- Make change a morally binding contract between your mind and soul.

- If you have too little time on your hands to complete too much work, rather than increase the pace, slow down.

- Just because your life has taken a wrong turn, it doesn't mean you have to end up in a cul-de-sac.

- The more you climb, the higher you'll reach.

- The tougher the mountain, the more fulfilling the climb and the more rewarding the view at the top.

- You don't have to be a giant to walk tall.

# chapter six
## from knock-backs to knock-outs

When I first started out in advertising, few would give me the time of day to look at my work. I remember once visiting the offices of McCann-Erickson, a London advertising agency considered at the time to be one of the most prestigious in town.

I had managed to get an appointment to meet a divisional creative director. (This in itself was an achievement – he was always notoriously busy.) As I had assumed, his office was on the penthouse floor of the building, huge and imposingly well-appointed.

He asked to look at my portfolio. As I hadn't yet had much practical experience, there was very little to show. I waited whilst he slowly flicked over the few laminated pages of my work. On closing my portfolio, he grimaced and motioned me over to the window from which he enjoyed a panoramic view of London,

*'Well Gabay,'* he said. *'Here's what I think. Do you see that man down there walking across the road?'*

*'Yes,'* I replied relishing the anticipation of the creative director's favourable and highly creative observation.

*'Do you know that man, have you ever met him before?*

*'No,'* I answered.

*'Well neither have I,'* replied the creative director.

*'But I can tell you this. Despite having just met you and never having met that guy, I bet he has more chance of making it in this business, as well as more creative ability in his little finger, than you will ever have in your*

*entire life. Now do me a favour you little shit, get out of my office, this business and everyone's life, NOW!'*

I stood outside McCann-Erickson's building, feeling shell-shocked. My options were clear. I could have either followed the creative director's advice and left the business pronto, or believed in myself to the point of proving him wrong.

I spent the ensuing months knocking on the doors of advertising agencies, begging for appointments. With hindsight, I am not quite sure where I found the courage to face rejections virtually on a daily basis. Yet, I kept on.

Eventually I landed a job as a junior copywriter. From that point, prospects began to improve slowly yet surely. Within a couple of years I became creative director, and then held a second creative directorship, as well as creative group head and similar executive positions in places like Hong Kong. It led to my being elected to the faculty of the world's largest marketing training body and writing several highly successful industry-leading textbooks on advertising and marketing.

So why did I do it? Was it simply to prove the creative director at McCann-Erickson wrong? Was I arrogant? Maybe. Was I obsessed? Unquestionably. Was I difficult to live with during the whole process? Without doubt! Above all, the experience taught me something totally unforeseen. I could have guessed at that time that to reinvent successfully, you need to believe in yourself and have an almost obsessive desire to overcome hurdles.

## Short-term knock-backs don't count – it's the final outcome that really matters.

But more importantly, and without trying to appear trite, it taught me that, with good health and the support of those who mean the most, you can attain greater achievements than you at first aspired towards.

For example, whilst achieving your career goals is always great, the sense of pride gained from having accomplished your aims, or at least having had a good go at achieving them, will always be magnified if you are surrounded by people who honestly appreciate your efforts. Better still, if having reached your goal, those close friends and family provide a purpose for enduring the entire rigmarole in the first place.

This takes on even greater significance if, having fought for what you once believed in, you discover that your goal wasn't all it was originally cracked up to be. Providing you can continue to draw on the strength of those who matter the most, and the belief, however seemingly faint, that you naturally harbour within yourself, then you can pursue an even higher cause. It may or may not be as financially rewarding as your original aim, but in any case, it could turn out to be more personally enriching.

Irrespective of where you decide to take your dream, stick to following your plans for reinvention – even if at first things appear hopelessly doomed to failure or, at the least, intrinsically testing. As an old saying goes: 'No amount of darkness can overcome the tiniest light.'

## You'll get by – just like them

If the road to hell is paved with good intentions, often the highway to success is tiled with mismatched stones that can easily cause the odd slip-up or two.

Just as my encounter with that creative director taught me an unexpected as well as priceless lesson, so I hope that you can draw lessons from some of the following examples of triumph over adversity and, more importantly, reinvention achievements:

◆ In 1947, legendary Hollywood sex goddess Marilyn Monroe was dismissed by Twentieth Century-Fox studios for being ugly!

◆ Joan of Arc, the much revered saint of the Roman Catholic church, who liberated Orléans from the English in 1492 and escorted the uncrowned Charles VII at his coronation, was totally illiterate.

◆ The much admired American sex therapist, Dr Ruth Westheimer, experienced two failed marriages.

◆ The Beatles, the world's most successful pop group, initially had their audition tape turned down by every leading record company in town.

◆ Despite having a doctorate in philosophy, Karl Marx, who founded democratic socialism and revolutionary communism, was refused a university teaching post.

◆ Mao Tse-Tung, ruler of the People's Republic of China from 1949 to 1976, changed careers after feeling rejected for not getting a top librarian's job.

◆ Jerry Seinfeld, whose own TV show became one of America's most successful situation comedy series of all time, used to tele-sale discount light bulbs and market fake jewellery.

◆ One of England's greatest footballers, Gary Lineker, believed that his destiny was to continue his family fruit and vegetable stall in Leicester.

◆ Don Bradman, one of the world's greatest cricketers, attributed his all-time batting record to 90 per cent concentration and 10 per cent skill. Need proof? As Don walked on to the field to bat on his last Test appearance at Lords cricket ground in London, the crowd and fellow players gave him such a tumultuous farewell ovation that he was clean bowled, first ball!

◆ Gloria Estefan, the international singing star, was at first an interpreter at Miami International airport.

◆ Al Pacino tried to make ends meet by becoming a delivery boy and later an usher and porter.

◆ Steven Spielberg, the brilliant film director, never made the grade to get into UCLA film school.

- In the literary world, Jane Austen's first novel was rejected, whilst her second was sold to a publisher who never published it.

- Charles Dickens, indisputably one of the world's most notable writers, dropped out of school when only 14 years old.

- F. Scott Fitzgerald, author of *The Great Gatsby* and other classic novels, failed in French, history and algebra at school and dropped out of university.

- In the world of science, Thomas Alva Edison, inventor of such things as the light bulb and typewriter, was sacked from his job in a local telegraph office after one of his experiments exploded. Later, when he became famous, a journalist asked him how he felt about having failed in so many experiments. He answered, 'I have not failed. I've just found 10,000 ways that didn't work.'

'Genius is 1 per cent inspiration and 99 per cent perspiration.'
Thomas Alva Edison

## *You* in action: the waiting game

During your working lifetime, you will probably change jobs and even careers at least five times. This is certainly not a failing on your part. Indeed, it is an integral part of your reinvention process and, given the right motives, it becomes one of your greatest attributes.

A training organization where I worked as a lecturer occasionally sent me to Leeds in the UK to deliver one-day talks on marketing and copywriting. Intermittently, by way of a gesture to the venue hosting the talks (a local hotel), the organizers allowed one or two hotel staff to sit in. On one such occasion, a waiter joined us.

In subsequent discussions, the waiter told me that he thought the whole business of writing adverts was great fun! He giggled at my examples of weird and wonderful adverts from around the world and enjoyed participating in class exercises; in fact much more than any of the other delegates whose everyday job remits included writing advertising copy.

At the end of the course the waiter shook my hand and thanked me, adding that he would be saving his tips to buy a PC with a fast Internet connection.

Some months later, I was back at Leeds for a talk on writing for the Internet in plain English. Although the course was full, I again allowed the waiter to listen in.

The waiter actively participated in the course. When it was over, he again thanked me, adding that he had bought the PC – a second-hand model and had started to study Web design and marketing. In fact, he had already designed a few pages for some friends, who in turn, had recommended him to others.

The last I heard was that the waiter had set up a small, yet busy Web design and marketing company. Good for him. A truly dedicated example of reinvention!

## Gravitate towards triumphant reinvention

Often when trying to bring about a change – especially one as radical as reinvention, you come up against what can appear as gigantic forces opposing your well-intentioned actions. The third of Sir Isaac Newton's Laws of Physics states that every action has an equal and opposite reaction. So, if you push on anything, it pushes back on you.

A force is a push or a pull upon an object, which comes about as a result of that object's interaction with another object. Some forces result from what are called contact interactions (e.g. tension or friction). Others result from distance interactions (e.g. gravity or magnetic forces).

You can spot action–reaction force pairs in nature. For example, a fish uses its fins to push water backwards. But a push on the water will only serve to accelerate the water. In turn, the water pushes the fish forward, propelling it through the water. For every action, there is an equal (in size) and opposite (in direction) reaction force. In this way, action–reaction force pairs make it possible for the fish to swim.

In terms of forces working against reinvention, consider the reaction of Hollywood actor George Clooney on how the British press was harassing Lady Diana, Princess of Wales. He publicly vowed never to court the press again, urging the public to see through their self-motivated interests.

Years later, George was back in London for the premiere of one of his movies. When he appeared at a press reception, the photographers laid down their cameras in protest. The mighty Clooney looked like a bemused and bewildered patient, straight out of the Emergency Room.

## Any action you take to change your life may meet an equally strong opposing reaction.

This doesn't mean that at the first hint of opposition you should just give up or recoil to a safer retreat. In fact, anything but …

When I applied Newton's Third Law to the example of throwing a ball, initially I felt that the Law didn't make any sense. Clearly, when I threw a ball, it wasn't returning the compliment and pushing me over. That's because there were many other forces involved. What's more, as each force came into play, it had an equal and opposite reaction on another.

This Law applied equally to the sheer impertinence of McCann-Erickson's creative director, whom I came to regard eventually as a nonentity; to this day I can't even remember his name. He certainly had more clout in the business than I. However, given the fact that I believed in my convictions, I was able to turn his energy ('force') against me into a propellent. The speed of my positive reaction was also affected by the fact that I didn't have anything to lose, whereas others had to maintain reputations, image and so on.

## Big isn't necessarily beautiful

Back to Newton, he taught that acceleration is dependent on both force and mass. If you are driving down a motorway at 70 mph and a bug hits your car's windscreen, clearly according to Newton's Third Law of Motion, the bug hits the windscreen and the windscreen hits the bug. Looking at the resulting state of the bug – splattered across the windscreen – compared to the windscreen still intact, you could be forgiven for believing that the windscreen had a greater action–reaction than the bug. In fact, they were equal in force. The fact that the bug was splattered across the windscreen only meant that its smaller mass made it less able to withstand the larger acceleration resulting from the interaction with the windscreen. But being small doesn't necessarily mean you lose out in a fight with a bigger, faster object.

When thinking about reinvention, often people dupe themselves into believing that if they are up against what on the outside at least, appears to be a bigger or tougher opponent, for example at the workplace, then they have little, if any chance of winning an argument. This is not necessarily true. After all, as I explained earlier, Newton's Third Law states that every action has an equal and opposite reaction. Getting what you want isn't just about the size of your opponent; it's more to do with the stature and solidity of your argument.

The more you plan for what you want and believe is right, by considering viable ways to express your message, the greater your chances of success.

If you were involved in two separate tug-of-war battles and pulled upon a rope first attached to a wall and then, in the second battle, the rope was held by Mr Universe, in each case the force would remain the same. You would only be able to pull so hard (and so the resisting force back would only be so big). The only variation would be your tactics to win the battle.

'However thinly you slice it, there are always two sides.'

Baruch Spinoza

The world is made up of different types of people – all pulling on ropes to get you to see issues from their perspective. Dealing with each type of person takes an exceptional understanding of their motives. Often such drives are on absolutely opposing sides of the divide.

## Take a walk in the boss's shoes

Try to recognize the probable state of mind of the people who behave badly towards you. In their position, with their own pressures, would you have honestly acted differently?

This can be particularly helpful when dealing, for example, with a difficult nit-picking boss. A negative boss invariably surrounds himself or herself with downbeat people. That's because unconstructiveness tends to rub off on everyone it comes into contact with. (Apart from people who love or care for the person who is broadcasting the negativity in the first place.)

It's all too easy to believe that the difficult boss is giving a free rein to direct their frustrations on you – and you alone. Yet once you begin to understand that they may well be stuck in a kind of role play, assuming the character of Mr or Mrs Demanding (some play it particularly well), you can see how it may be difficult for them to step out of that temperament. In fact you might even begin to feel sorry for them.

The status of such types of bosses may have landed them in a nice office suite from which they can look down at the people below (such a lonely and miserable feeling, seeing only the top of people's heads, and never connecting face-to-face). It's one of the main grievances with being the person where the buck stops. Often such people, including CEOs, are respected, but not necessarily liked. For them reinvention is often about getting to grips with their personal performance as a leader rather than solely their presentation as a figurehead.

So rather than getting flustered, use their demands to your benefit. Convert their apparent negativity into enthusiasm, enabling you to move forward. Show that you are focused on the way ahead, rather than what has come before. It's not just a case of being visionary in an abstract sense, but of using constructive, as well as expressive, language to get your views across: the project wasn't simply 'okay' it was *'fun'*. Or: 'the meeting didn't quite go to plan, however, at least it provided some useful tips on how to better handle a difficult situation the next time around.' Providing you don't come across as insincere (all smiles – whatever the climate), once enthusiasm takes root, it will outgrow even the most die-hard of negative thinkers. What's more, in the process it will help them feel more connected to the team whilst improving everyone's performance.

If, on the other hand, having taken the time to understand why things happened, you still feel justified to be annoyed, go ahead – it's your right. But at least your annoyance will be grounded in reasoning and your subsequent actions will be forged by insight of both your aggressors and you, the aggrieved.

## The battle of logic against belligerence

It's not just difficult bosses who may try and stand in the way of your reinvention. The contenders for 'heavyweight champions of impediment' are many. Rather than attempting to deliver a strong knock-out blow by punching at them in all directions, try to understand their motives.

### THEY JAB

**The box jelly-fish** They will travel a million miles to find fault in everyone – especially *you*. Once they have spotted a fault – be it real or fabricated – to meet their purposes, they will unsettle you and try and keep you pinned to the ground.

### YOU KNOCK OUT

Let them pin you! However, whilst you are on the ground, have a word in their ears about how their 'advice' is appreciated and how you have a proposal that will make everyone come out as champs – especially them.

### THEY JAB

**The weathered workers** They hang around the company vending machine, bitching and whining about how the boss did 'this' to them or the client had the audacity to do 'that'.

### YOU KNOCK OUT

Don't become like water, which cleans away dirt but, in the process, becomes muddy. Rather than joining in the moaning, sympathize with their cause. However, at the same time, through example show how they could rise above the squalor of politics – especially politics at work.

### THEY JAB

**The walls have ears** If you have worked for any length of time in an office, you will definitely have come across this type. They'll let you – and ostensibly, you alone – into a secret about the boss, employee or anyone else that they care to pick on. Within a very short time, it becomes crystal clear that they have shared a similar secret with just about everyone else in the office – only this time the subject of their gossip is you.

### YOU KNOCK OUT

Learn from standard military tactics: cause a diversion. For example, Mary in accounts tells Peter in the IT department that she found out his boss was thought to be moonlighting. Rather than getting drawn into this conjecture by passing on the information – which, as in any closed environment such as an office, will eventually end up in the ears of the Boss, nod in awe at Mary's deviousness, but take it no further. Often, before you speak you are the master of your words. However once you speak – especially if you don't check your facts, words become your master – you'll spend most of your energy trying to either cover them up or justifying why you opened your mouth in the first place!

## THEY JAB

**But-Heads** These are close cousins to the 'However' family. You'll commonly meet them at committee meetings. Each time you come up with even a half-way sensible idea, they clear their vocal chords, sit upwards and yell, 'BUT!!!!' Variations of their call include:

◆ That's impossible.

◆ Believe me I would be the first to help – but it's not my department.

◆ Fantastic – ingenious – but no way.

◆ It's radical, I can see that but it's a bit too extreme.

◆ Now, come on. Do you honestly call that an idea?

◆ I love it, but will everyone really love it? Nah.

◆ It will never work.

◆ It's been done before.

◆ Let's sleep on it.

◆ It's never been done before – so why start now?

◆ It's too expensive to achieve.

◆ It's not the way we do things around here.

◆ Stop dreaming.

◆ Wake up and smell the coffee.

◆ I am going to keep this one in my top drawer. When the market's ready, just hang on to my coat tails and we'll let this one fly.

## YOU KNOCK OUT

Empathize, clearly showing you understand their view. Then draw upon facts, rather than opinion alone, to show why you disagree with those views. Bearing in mind that you don't have to be disagreeable to disagree, work with 'But-Heads' to turn those closed minded 'buts' into open-ended 'Howevers'.

**List managers** These people seemingly place your needs at the top of their list of things to do. However, for commercial/personal/financial / political/reasons (which you'll know when they decide that you need to know – not right now), your needs never get round to being met. Which is not surprising as they have so many other 'commitments' already on their little list.

David in production is growing desperate. He needs authority for a new printing machine. Every time he brings up the issue with his manager, he is told that the Board is aware of the need to upgrade equipment and has even listed it as a priority. (No one from the Board has spoken directly to David about this.) For the time being, however, David must simply work harder to get more out of his existing equipment.

Rather than just blindly accept this and the consequences of an unreliable printer, David sends a memo to the boss – detailing the instruction and possible reasonable short-term measures. Then when the machine inevitably packs up, rather than the boss turning round and blaming David for not having dealt with the matter earlier, by using the evidence, David can prove to both his boss and the Board that he complied with the instructions, even suggesting alternatives to a costly printing machine.

He would thereby have demonstrated his initiative, understanding and co-operation – fine management material for the 'powers at the top' to chew over.

**I'm on your side – really** These confident, softly spoken, universally admired 'unassuming' pullers argue that under different circumstances they would be the first to help you. However, using the excuse that 'it is not an ideal world', *you* had better start helping *them*!

## YOU KNOCK OUT

It will soon become apparent that the world under the 'unassuming' dictatorship of this group will never be a comfortable place, let alone Utopia. Unless you make the move out of their world – even if that move is made as graciously as their untenable demands – you will end up forever thanking them for consistently punching you in the face.

## THEY JAB

**Mr/Ms Ideal** These rope-pullers demand that the rope has golden tassels at both ends. They and everything about them is so flawless and lavish that you too feel socially inadequate. Worse and more perverse still, as time goes by, they use the rope to flog themselves rather that just thrash you. After all, for a perfectionist, the person most flawed will always be himself or herself. Indeed, for them life is like an onion, which is peeled layer by layer – each providing a further reason to weep.

## YOU KNOCK OUT

There are times when the best thing you can do for people is offer compassion but go no further. Whilst for many, perfection can never be achieved, your task is to face the reality of your own reinvention rather than worry about what should or should not be corrected. Leave the futility of finding errors in everything to autocrats with little else to do with their lives than gaze in mirrors all day to spot flaws.

## THEY JAB

**The Reclusives** This couple feel they have spent the best years of their lives making sacrifices. They resent the world. It's time for you to pay for everyone's sins, even if you are just an innocent bystander. In their eyes you are the official representative of everyone they have ever had the wretched pleasure to deal with. So, step up to the noose and wait for the ground to fall from your feet.

It's strange how, despite knowing that the ground is going to open beneath their feet, when it will open and where precisely to stand, many don't simply step aside. There will always be the Victor Meldrews and Mr and Ms Angry from Little Town. Their gloom is like a black hole. Just as a black hole sucks in everything around itself, so even the most cheery reinventor can feel drawn into their despondency. As soon as you spot their presence, step aside. The more you deal with these characters, the harder it will become to escape their pessimism and ultimately your own downfall.

**Drama Queens** For these people, problems are not simply bad, they are desperate. Equally, when things go well, they offer so much praise that you'll think you've been press-ganged into joining the local gospel choir.

When dealing with Drama Queens, you'll want to use your rope as an escape device to lower you down their tower of shame/fame (depending on their mood — which is forever changing).

**Guilt-givers** Ostensibly the last thing these rope pullers want is for you to feel in any way guilty about the considerable sacrifices made on your behalf. These range from giving you your first lucky break, to paying your monthly wage, to covering up for your ineptitude (usually brought about through following their instructions) — even, in the case of a parent, to giving you life. As a Guilt-giver would put it, 'Go ahead, enjoy yourself, have a great time. Don't even give a moment's thought about me taking on what are arguably your responsibilities. After all, that's the reason that I was put onto this earth — so that you can reap the rewards, whilst I remain in the shadows. In return, if you do happen to have some spare time on your trip to Utopia, could you get me a small commemorative mug of your journeys? Here's the money to pay for it.'

## YOU KNOCK OUT

Ask yourself why Guilt-givers go through so many hoops to make their point. You'll probably find that it boils down to wanting to be acknowledged and appreciated. However, probably not in a flamboyant sort of way, but when the opportunity arises for them to step out of character for a few moments, you will be on hand to listen without their fearing having all that guilt thrown back. That's when together you can reinvent your prospects.

## THEY JAB

**Till Death Do Us Part**  These rope-pullers are more akin to rope-*pushers*. They count amongst the hardest of all people to deal with. Whatever you want to achieve, they slavishly go along with it. Want to make them work all night to get a project completed? No problem and they won't even take a five-minute loo break. These people can get in your way by giving you insufficient space to breathe, let alone act.

## YOU KNOCK OUT

Just because they say they can handle extra responsibilities, it doesn't mean that you should feel obliged to overburden them. Allow them to complete each project before moving on to the next. In both the short and long term everyone will gain and feel more confident to move on to deal with more challenging projects, leading to even more rewarding reinvention.

## THEY JAB

**Respect your elders**  These people have years of experience pulling and pushing the right ropes. Having sat dutifully at their feet, listening to them drone on and on like some Eastern mystic, you conclude that to all intents and purposes they have reached supernatural levels of understanding. So you feel obliged to pay close attention to every syllable spoken. Yet, the more you try to adapt their advice to match your reinvention plans, the more they believe you are ignoring it.

Your best tactic when dealing with this group is to skip to their rope – but at your own pace.

**Political Posers** As with anyone wanting your vote of confidence, these rope-pullers will offer any image you wish, in order to impress and so win you over to their philosophy and strategies.

Beware of their motives, but don't become cynical. For example, I worked at a company that always ensured that their best team worked on new business projects. Once the project was secured, it was handed over to another team to deal with on an ongoing basis. Arguably, clients could have said that the company's motives were very short term and demand that the original team should continue any project work. However, on closer examination it clearly made sense to offer an initial injection of high dynamism and sustain the momentum with a team able to devote time to developing not only the initial project, but a working relationship. If, on reinventing yourself, you come across people who seem exceptionally keen to support your venture, remember to hope for the best, but plan for the probable.

## Try and see it my way

And now for a little confession. I have always admired the Greek sage Socrates, whose axiom was 'Know yourself'. With this in mind I can reveal that a little part of each of the individual rope-puller classifications is in fact me. I wonder how much of them is also a part of *you* and the people you know? My tactic in dealing with each type of person is reinforced through my ability to deal with myself.

My late father would say 'Even a king or chairman of a multinational conglomerate has to go to the loo'. In short, the people who anger you or whom you fear most on account of their status are, at the end of the day, just as vulnerable as you. Turn your anger into compassion without turning yourself into a wimp. Recognize that people, irrespective of veneers, are just people with all that that entails.

## Corporate rope-pullers

Just as I have listed various individual rope-pullers, so I believe that from the point of view of a career reinventor, you should be aware of different corporate types. I have arrived at them through comparing each type to a culturally self-determining community. Broadly, these communities are culturally measured according to *how* they do what they do (their technology, infrastructure and so on) and *why* they do what they do (mission goals and management values).

As with all cultural divides, differences can lead to fragmentation. Which is why it pays in your choice of employer to match your ideology to the kind of organization that you want to be associated with.

My corporate rope-pullers:

◆ *Heritage is everything* These corporations – and most often institutions – live and in due course die by their long heritage, however antiquated.

◆ *Jazz players* These corporations have a strong core set of values and product/service direction, yet are willing to experiment into new areas.

◆ *Climbers* These corporations encourage people to work themselves up or across the ranks. For them, status is everything.

◆ *Crystal gazers* These corporations go out of their way to secure stability through planning and adjusting expectations.

◆ *Lions* These macho corporations strive to reach goals – however far-fetched those aims may be.

◆ *Lionesses* These more 'feminine' corporations aim at encouraging internal as well as external market harmonization between the organization and everyone who comes in contact with it.

- *Tamers* These corporations are like lion tamers – constantly balancing the needs of both lions and lionesses.

- *Wolves* These corporations encourage individuality as well as team building. In this way, they are like wolf packs – rearing the individual team member in preparation for the group conquest of assignments.

Whatever tactic you adopt when faced with individual or corporate rope-pullers stop and think first. If you rush to weigh up a problem at face value, you might find you've acted without considering all the motives, politics and individual circumstances behind the problem. First consider: Why has this arisen? Why is this person behaving this way? You'll deal with it much better as a result.

## Know when to act

Prior to Glasnost and Perestroika, in order to survive in the Russian Communist Party one had to learn when to act for or against the Party; or indeed when to just bide time collecting interesting titbits of information that one day could prove useful. It's the same in capitalist corporate life. If someone at work with the right connections at a senior level causes your demotion simply because a person has worked in the company far longer than you and uses the connections to sabotage all your good work, forgive the little 'govniuk' then move on. (Remember, I said forgive, not forget.)

Stop trying to summon up excuses for such unethical behaviour. Think of it like this: If you buy a litre of milk and, despite the fact that it looks fresh, the milk is soured, you naturally pour it away. By the same token, if someone is behaving sourly towards you, always promising one thing but instead doing the opposite, stop making excuses. The milk is off, that's it, chuck it!

Often when you are stuck in a rut you become unfocused. You know you want to improve your standing at work or at home, yet someone stands in your way. Confront the dilemma rather than dwell on it. Pinpoint the actions that have made you unfocused. Remember that for every action there is an opposing reaction, so use that force to scupper your opponent.

In fact, imagine how much more focused you could become about reinvention if you could simply let slip through your fingers redundant grievances concerning people who 'if only they didn't do this' or 'if only they could have done that ...'

## The more you remain focused on your goals, the greater your depth of thought.

The whole process starts by thinking about becoming focused. So stop allowing your mind to wander and start focusing on something to wonder about!

A wise man once told me that it is best to have lots of little worries rather than just one big anxiety. Why? 'Because if you have lots of little worries to deal with, your mind doesn't get stuck in a rut, obsessing over one big issue and never dealing with others, which tend to mount up anyway.'

## *You* in action: from MP to much published

I asked Edwina Currie, a former English Member of Parliament, now a highly successful novelist and broadcaster, whether she felt that people are driven to continually reinvent themselves.

Most people settle happily in a routine, which becomes a rut, and are jogged out of it only by disaster, such as redundancy, illness and the like. Whenever these sorts of things happen, along with kids leaving home, serious sports injuries and of course a spouse dying or separating or just becoming boring, then 'now' becomes the perfect time to reinvent yourself. That takes a very positive frame of mind.

Did Edwina feel that she had truly reinvented herself?

These days I ask the questions rather than answer them. However, there are loads of connections, not least the skill of the wordsmith, common to all three professions.

Edwina believes that the reinvention process never stops, and I totally agree with her.

It's fun and useful to adapt to changing times and circumstances. Women do it better than men. Also, you don't have to be religious to reinvent yourself. Having faith in yourself is what's needed.

'You are the storyteller of your own life, and you can create your own legend or not.'

Isabel Allende, novelist

Whilst the world will always have people ready to gaze down from their seemingly secure, lofty towers and dismiss any potential that could possibly blossom, there will be even more people who will rise above common expectations through resolute flair and aptitude.

Believe me, if such people – be they rich, poor, inspired, determined, rebellious, down-trodden, uplifted, renowned, self-effacing or reclusive – can reinvent themselves, then so can you.

## REINVENTING YOU

◆ Value your health and the support of family and friends.

◆ Make negative forces thrust your reinvention plans forward.

◆ Your argument for reinvention is as solid as your conviction for it.

◆ Think strategically, act tactically.

◆ Act tactically, tactfully.

◆ You don't have to be disagreeable to disagree.

◆ For every action there is an opposing reaction: use that force to scupper your opponent.

- However thinly you slice your argument for reinvention, remember there will always be two sides to consider.

- Get to understand others' motives and they will begin to appreciate yours.

- Even your greatest adversary is as vulnerable to insecurity as you.

- Understand what makes your employer tick.

- Support your boss – but not at the cost of going against what you sincerely believe can benefit everyone.

- It's not where you start, it's where you finish that counts – and you haven't finished.

- You don't have to be a saint to turn anger into compassion.

- You have the right to be annoyed at people.

- Never apologize for being yourself.

- You don't have to take everyone's advice, but you pay the consequences of not listening to it.

- It's up to you to choose the degree of significance paid to any given situation.

- Reinvent beliefs that once made you miserable and you can start to change your life.

- You might find 10,000 ways of doing something wrong but it doesn't mean you've had 10,000 failures.

# chapter seven
## the past, the present and you

reinvent yourself

Idling away your present through incessantly reflecting over the past in a desperate hope that it can reveal your future can be pitiless and often pointless. In the book by J.K. Rowling, *Harry Potter and the Philosopher's Stone*, the hero, Harry Potter comes across a magnificent mirror set in an ornate golden frame perched on two clawed feet. The story relates how men wasted away just staring spellbound at this 'Mirror of Erised'. The mirrored image was the innermost, most forlorn desires of the heart. The most contented person in the world saw himself or herself exactly as they thought they were. Others, though, saw what they yearned for but would never hold – as reaching into the mirror would simply shatter the illusion.

Sometimes looking in the mirror can be painful …

'Why should I accept that I am uncooperative at work and could, if I really wanted to, compromise occasionally on certain things? Instead I want to dwell on the fact that my team-mates are difficult to work with, and my relationship with them will always be that way.'

'Why should I sit down with my partner to discuss why our relationship is going wrong? I am just stuck with that person's eccentricities. It comes with the unassailable, yet clause-riddled contract called "marriage".'

'Why should I forgive people for having been callous and indifferent to me?'

And so it goes on … Unless you are honest with yourself that the only one preventing you from taking appropriate action might be that person in the mirror, you could end up one day regretting what you should have done with your life rather than celebrating what you actually did.

## Just as you live with a quandary, so you possess the means to solve it.

To delve into a problem, manage it – face it full on. It doesn't mean you have to relish the pain that a problem brings. Neither does it mean that in order to gain something, you have to endure the anguish of a baptism by fire. (Life is difficult enough without looking for additional problems to burn your fingers on.) Emotional pain serves a purpose. Without it, you lose the challenge of confrontation. Even on the physical level, without pain, you might never know you were hurt.

Equally, when it come to changing your circumstances, the only one who can sentence you to serve the rest of your life in a dead-end job or a dead-end relationship is yourself. What's more, unless you make the change, everyone around you, especially those who care, will have to live with the ghost of your sufferance rather than help you move on to a brighter future.

Once you acknowledge reality, you can at least attempt to deal with any situation. The important thing is to make such a start, perhaps patiently – even modestly – and even if those issues are atrocious.

## Love hurts

Many are determined to scupper any chances of reinvention, even if it causes them pain. For example, I knew a guy who was determined to date a certain girl, but she didn't fancy him. Not because he was ugly but because he was just too nice!

Apparently, when she was very young, her father used to beat her up. As an adult she found that she couldn't sustain a lasting relationship with men. Of the men that she did date, curiously, she was drawn like a magnet to those who were more aggressive in nature. For her it was natural to be treated brutally.

It wasn't that she wanted 'a bit of rough' as an echo of her turbulent upbringing. It went far deeper. She invited violence so that she would be forced to bring the relationship to a traumatic close. However desperately a nice guy would try to convince her otherwise, she would continue her search for the abusers just to reaffirm her own victimization.

What goes round tends to come around. Ask any tyrant: it is far easier to pass on pain than to apportion pleasure. This is especially true if you pass back that pain to yourself which, coincidently, serves to aggravate your original feelings of oppression, malice and unfair treatment.

## Stop setting yourself up

Often because the past was horrendous, people set up ideals of what they should and ought to be, based on changing what they once were. For example, I saw an American chat-show which featured teenagers who were once considered as 'dorks' by all who knew them. This kind of 'label' drove the teenagers to reinvent themselves to such an extent that any remaining vestiges of who they once were became obliterated.

As is typical with many chat-shows, the programme featured a wacky title: 'From Dork to Wow!' The teenagers' antagonists who had never met them since school, were re-introduced on the programme to the teenagers who had ditched their so-called 'dorky' spectacles and hairstyles to become … *Super-smoothies*! They were toned … They were slick … They had the best educational qualifications. They were ready for the fast lane, and the only 'dorks' still hanging on to old thinking were the 'do-dos' who were once their adversaries.

Although their change was commendable, it seemed that the teenagers' bitterness over the past had compelled them to change only partially their way of life. This sort of thinking works against people in many ways. For example, you could decide to scale career heights just to compensate for your past. In itself, this is not a bad thing. However, if you become so self-obsessed that rather than improve matters, your attitude simply compels you to shove aside anyone who might stand in the way of your greatness – just as you too once were pushed aside – then all you will have achieved is to repeat history, rather than reinvent circumstances.

Just as one event leads to another, so the psychological step of coming to terms with your past may offer you a renewed sense of purpose to reinvent your future.

Perhaps for as long as you can recall, you have been labelled as a certain type of person. Rather than defend yourself, you decide that to make life easier, you might as well go along with perpetuating the legend. In the process, however, the fable becomes fact – or at least, it appears that way to others. The trouble with this, is that come the day you want people to see beyond the facade, you'll begin to wonder who you once were before the whole legend first propagated itself.

In many instances, especially if you count yourself amongst driven fast-laners in their twenties and thirties, perceptions of what you want to become are shaped by what you have been previously. For example, if you were the girl or boy who sat at the back of the class, too shy to answer questions, and no one at the time ever offered you the break you deserved, you may feel that remaining a doormat is your destined role in life. Worse still, you perpetuate that belief in yourself and others.

In many cases people who have had a rough upbringing often look cynically at the future. Whereas people who as children were spoilt, being given anything they asked for, often find it difficult to come to terms with the fact that as they grow older they don't always get what they want! Recognizing your own past is essential when dealing with changes. Whilst reinvention requires you to acknowledge the past, of greater importance is the fact that you live in the present and need to plan for the future.

'Now if there's a smile on my face, it's only there trying to fool the public.'

Smokey Robinson and the Miracles

Jenny, aged 28 and single, worked in the sales department of a telecommunications department. She was bright and believed that, in terms of 'closing a deal', she was not only as good as her male colleagues – she was better. To a great extent, she put it down to her looks. Ever since school, she had earned a reputation for getting what she wanted – especially from guys. Yet as a child, although always popular, she often felt lonely.

Now she had matured, Jenny felt she had learnt how to exploit the very thing that had made her popular by subtly using her charisma to secure her place at the top of the department sales ranks.

A particularly important contract was up for grabs. Jenny wanted to seize the opportunity. So she flirted mildly with the potential client, who didn't take the bait. This annoyed her. So, without becoming brazen, she became more blatantly flirtatious. Still nothing. As it happened, the contract was eventually won by a competitor.

A spiral of similar events led to Jenny losing every deal. Fearing that her colleagues would start to gossip that 'Jenny had lost her touch', she set out to prove that she still 'had it'. The only problem was her misconstrued interpretation of the word 'it'. The outcome was a series of one-night stands with the guys from the office. In the end, Jenny still had her reputation intact. However, through harking back to what had worked in the past, rather than seeking to utilize the full range of her gifts in the present, she became as bitter about herself and her colleagues as that lonely girl in the playground.

You can probably recognize variations of Jenny's story in characters at your own office. These include:

◆ *The office clown* Always good for a laugh except when others seem to ignore his or her personal opinions.

- *The office whiz-kid* The first 'port of call' to sort out any crisis. However, the only ship berthed at the harbour whilst the others have steered out to explore his or her suggested new opportunities.

- *The office furniture* Been at the office for years. Now part of the furniture, which tends to mean that although nice to have around, his or her ideas get 'sat on'. So much that this person ends up feeling saggy at the seams.

- *The office punch-ball* Tells everyone else that he or she has seen it all, done it all, and secured exclusive rights to the t-shirt. Everyone is offered an open invitation to deliver yet another blow to the person's esteem, ego, feelings or whatever else seems to be a good target to take people's minds off their own problems. Having endured so many kicks in the past, the person becomes impervious to everything – including pain.

## Stepping into the light

I spoke to two people who, in the past, had suffered serious abuse and I asked how they had coped.

The first was now a successful, 30-year-old professional, who had been a rape victim.

The most important thing I have learnt is that it is possible to learn to trust again. I will always be moving forward. It's up to me to take those steps. In the last few years I have learnt a lot about myself – or should that be about the reinvented person I have become? I now see that it was in many ways a mistake not to 'deal' with it at the time. I just had to wait until I was ready.

I have also accepted that it is possible to come out of a very dark place and see the light again. Each and every one of us has access to the bricks we need to build ourselves up again – but we have to force ourselves not to use those bricks to build a wall around us. Learning to trust is one of the hardest things to do, but it is a start for a better future.

I would like to put back some of the good work that has gone into getting me where I am today – not that carefree 22-year-old who suffered in silence, but a much wiser, 30-year-old, reinvented person.

The second person was an ex-paratrooper who years earlier underwent a serious assault in a pub.

Many things happen to us and often we decide that life is just not worth pursuing. If people let others know how they felt inside, they would realize that there are individuals out there who can help. If you don't ask in this life, you don't get. Too many people are just too frightened to re-live problems.

What advice did he have for those struggling to face their past?

Think of your problem as a clock face. There are different areas on a clock face: one to three, three to six, six to nine and nine to twelve. You have to go right the way round the clock face to get better. If you go to three o'clock and then jump to nine o'clock, missing six o'clock – the painful area – you'll never make it. Whilst time is a great healer, the best moment to start healing or if you like, reinventing, is the present.

It doesn't matter how severe or minor is your own pain when compared to someone else's. The fact that you are suffering is enough to warrant your wanting to improve the situation.

# Stop!

Negative self-fulfilling prophecy is one of the greatest stumbling blocks in any pursuit of reinvention. The only way to prevent divination is simply to stop doing the things that ultimately hurt.

'To keep trying the same thing over and over with the expectation of a different result is the definition of insanity.'

Albert Einstein

Suddenly just to stop doing what you are used to is easier said than done. One of the best ways to get around self-fulfilling prophecies is to forgive the person who placed you in your current state of mind.

Now don't panic! It doesn't mean that you have to don 'the good cloth', set up a portable confession booth, invite your antagonist over for tea, and recite a couple of Hail Mary's. Instead try to think a little more deeply about your relationships. If that antagonist turns out to be yourself, then even better.

## From penthouse to penitentiary

The convicted perjurer Lord Jeffrey Archer, once a virtuoso politician and enduring prolific writer able to turn a prison sentence into a compelling piece of prose, in effect epitomizes the meaning of *negative* reinvention.

Perhaps Archer's incapacity to reinvent himself in a positive way is shown by his apparent insincerity when it came to embracing change – even when he had asked for it. For example, in an interview with the respected journalist Thomas O'Dwyer, he asked for advice on a suitable name for an Irishman in a story. O'Dwyer said that Archer's idea for the name Shawn was stereotyped. 'Try Dermot, it's ethnically authentic. Dermot and Grainne were tragic lovers in a classic Celtic saga.' 'Dermot!' barked Archer, 'Wonderful!' When the book was published it featured an Irish character named Shawn.

In one of my earlier books, *The Meaning of Life,* Archer told me that he followed two maxims:

'The heights by great men reached and kept were not attained by sudden flight, but they, while their companions slept, were toiling upward in the night' (Henry Wadsworth Longfellow, 1807–82).

'Energy plus talent, you're a King, energy plus no talent, you're a Prince, talent and no energy, you're a pauper.'

Archer's energy was legendary. However, having energy alone, whilst ignoring advice to consider how best to direct that energy, invariably achieves little more than transitory solutions rather than enduring change.

## A league of gentlemen

Brian used to work as a courier. Through no fault of his own, he developed a brain tumour. Day after day in a nursing home he would shout in desperation. He felt imprisoned by his condition. 'Why me, why me?' He had been told his condition was fatal. When I visited him in the home, initially I was at a loss for words. I tried to get his mind off things by talking about his job. Prior to being a courier he had worked for the local council as a road-layer.

As he answered some of my questions such as 'how long does it take for tarmac to set?' he calmed down. I also noticed an autographed photo of the Manchester United football team hanging on his wall, along with a letter from Sir Alex Ferguson, the team mentor. Sir Alex had heard of Barry's condition and in his letter wished Barry well and thanked him for his support.

That one letter gave Barry a tremendous lift. I bet it also helped put any problems that Sir Alex might have had into perspective.

All these ordeals highlight something that affects a much wider group of people (perhaps including you) who, when facing unforeseen challenges, hope to resolve their problems through reinvention. When the unexpected strikes, you might say 'It hit me out of the blue – like a thunderbolt'. Just as a thunderbolt lights up the sky, so adversity, when properly managed, can be overcome, at least partially, through determination and support.

**Adversity can re-energize your resolve to accomplish what might otherwise have seemed impossible.**

## Value yourself

Albert Bandura developed a psychological concept called *self-efficacy*. It dealt with how people judge their capacity to cope in various situations. Everyone's self-efficacy level changes according to circumstance. It explains why sometimes you feel 'cool' about something, whilst at other times you feel completely out of your depth.

The way you can evaluate your own self-efficacy is often down to your personal experiences: you are either familiar with handling a situation or you are not. To an even greater extent, self-efficacy is dependent upon the encouragement offered by other people to help you manage that situation. As with many aspects of reinvention, it's all a matter of confidence – offering it, taking it, using it and sharing it.

## The right coping strategy for change

In the workplace there are, broadly speaking, four types of changes.

1 *Gradual change*  This manifests itself either very slowly over time or in subtle fluctuations in force. This kind of change is typified in companies that have an open-ended strategy of on going growth.

2 *Radical change*  This is a dramatic, abrupt kind of change. It could manifest itself through relocation, entering new markets, changing fundamental policies and so on.

3 *Crisis change*  This is when immediate, if not drastic, measures are called for to avoid overall ruin. In dealing with crisis change within an organization, typically one person or a small team of people with power and knowledge are sanctioned to establish a critical need and resolve it through quick-witted negotiation with everyone affected by the crisis. Whilst this kind of quick-fix change is the most common, it is also the most futile. One averted calamity usually turns out to be just a short-term answer to what is often a much bigger, if not complex, issue.

4 *Developmental change*  This is when, for example, a small business grows bigger and at a much faster rate than first assumed. Without advance planning for growth, the organization would ultimately collapse. Another example of developmental change is when an event overtakes circumstances; like the public deciding to buy from shopping malls instead of corner shops. Whenever

developmental change takes place, it invariably calls for people to learn new skills, which in reinvention terms, is constructive.

Providing that you remain adaptable and handle change as part of a greater challenge rather than confront an isolated project as an end in itself, any change that brings direct or even indirect benefits is a change for the better. Yet to do so you have to remain focused on coping with immediate issues and wider implications. Coping with changes – whether at work or at home – may well bring its own set of concerns.

## Strategies for change

Psychologists suggest that there are two kinds of coping strategies when dealing with change. First, *problem-focused strategies*, which deal with the immediate environment. For example, asking for advice from others who have gone through similar experiences or adopted a different practical approach to the issue in question.

The second coping strategy is the *emotion-focused strategy*, in which you try to rethink and so reframe your instinctive reaction and response to a situation. You may just take a few deep breaths, relax and then review the problem when you are in a calmer state of mind. The trouble is that some issues of reinvention need direct action rather than philosophical digression.

Sadly, there are even times when you may have to deal with changes that are unchangeable. For example, according to NHS figures, up to 30 per cent of adults in the UK have to cope with chronic illness. At first they try to understand their illness including its symptoms and degree of pain or severity. Next, they may find themselves panicking as it becomes clear that the illness just won't go away. This is when the support of family and friends is essential. Third, they may turn to medical or complementary means. Finally they realize they have to accept the change and, depending on their level of self-efficacy, either agonize over their ultimate fate or learn to live for the moment, irrespective of what each day will bring.

# A price worth paying?

In a world where just about everything from cradle to grave has a price, there is also a hidden cost to pay for perceiving what things may *purport* to be rather than what they in fact are. Psychologists call this a 'cognitive cost'. 'Cognitive' covers matters such as thinking, perceiving and problem solving.

Ulric Neisser defined cognition as the processes 'by which the sensory input is transformed, reduced, elaborated, stored, recovered, and used'. In this way, 'cognition is involved in everything a human being might possibly do'.

Cognitive cost drives people to conclusions, based on their initial reading of a situation. For example, imagine Microsoft announcing the launch of an innovative computer operating system that was so simple to use, even a 10-year-old would have no problem in grasping the technology. Let's say that their marketing convinced you to buy the software. Yet on opening the packaging, you discover a training manual so large that it could be used as a door-stop!

Cognitive costs theory suggests that simply by looking at the size of the manual you could assume that, rather than being child's play, to understand the entire operating system requires the mind of a genius. In other words, you have literally judged the book by its cover.

Especially in the field of packaging design, understanding this kind of view can quite literally shape how a product or service concept is communicated to the buying public.

Irrespective of whether you work for a trendy design agency or IT company, often during your working career you become so immersed in the business of reinventing products and services for commercial purposes, that you start to climb a metaphorical ladder supported by perceptions rather than substance.

# When climbing the reinvention ladder, make sure you have a firm footing.

## It's got to be perfect

The fruitless occupation of climbing unsteadily Jacob's ladder to reach idyllic states of reinvention doesn't apply solely to adults. As a child you may have been encouraged to reach top grades in class. Failure may have resulted in anything from a reassuring 'just try to do better next time' to a smack. Irrespective of the approach taken, a child can panic on learning of the low grade. Without the reassurance of parental support, the child could fear an imagined fate ranging from excruciating torture to being packed off in a spaceship to Mars!

When communication between child and parent goes really off beam, even greater problems can crop up. For example, in some cases, the child could become obsessive about getting school work absolutely right, at any cost. It often happens that when children who have consistently been top of the class receive unexpected lower grades, they interpret the results as a fall from grace. Net result: everything needs to be restored to perfection. That can bring about real anger and frustration within themselves. In the most severe instances that anger can manifest itself in anything from withdrawal and depression to self-mutilation. Sometimes they take their cue from their peers on how best to escape from the perceived annoyance and small-minded thinking of parents, teachers and the system in general. That in turn can lead to anything from general indifference to any difficult situation to rebelliousness expressed via drug-taking, promiscuity, etc.

## Your world according to Wundt

You don't have to be a kid to feel frustrated with the world. Adults frequently feel angry and frustrated about not attaining what, at least in their eyes, is perfection. I mentioned in a previous chapter Mr and Mrs Ideal, for whom flawless reinvention would appear unattainable. Psychologically speaking, such characters often view the world from the point of view of Wilhelm Wundt.

Wundt (1832–1920) was accredited with establishing the science of modern psychology. He taught that people should become introspective and study their own mental state. On the other hand, his critics argued that studying your own mental state all day long would drive you nuts! Mind you, it could also steer you to the nearest psychologist's surgery. (Maybe, from a commercial viewpoint at least, Wundt's ideas weren't that 'mad' after all!)

When perfectionists look at an issue, they isolate each part of the whole picture. For them, reinvention projects can never be concluded to total satisfaction. In fact, the effecting of each assignment (part of a project) achieves no more than an end within itself. In this way, small projects always remain diminutive, irrespective of the potential for greater achievements.

## Bits and pieces of a bigger jigsaw

On the other hand, perhaps you aspire to be one of the great reinventors who tend to assess questions from a Gestalt viewpoint. That is, they look at the form, shape and pattern of something as a whole rather than just parts.

Gestalt psychology was developed in Germany during the early part of the last century. Max Wertheimer (1880–1943) is credited with founding it. He argued that people shouldn't seek to understand human behaviour by breaking it down into fragments but offered a set of principles to illustrate how perceptions are structured into meaningful wholes.

One of the best ways to understand this is to visit a major city centre like London's Piccadilly Circus or New York's Times Square. Both venues are renowned for their advertising hoardings, often featuring a cascade of moving lights. Although the effect of the lights is fluid movement, in actuality, the movement is created by individual light bulbs being switched on and off at around 60 millisecond intervals. Similarly, successful reinventors appreciate that unless each 'light' (that is, a step towards what they aspire to achieve) is switched either on or off in sequence, the total effect of fluid, positive movement towards a bright future will never be reached.

## Building a perceptual pyramid

Reaching your goals at work or at home can often be achieved through motivating a series of successful steps.

In 1970, one of the twentieth-century's greatest psychologists died. Abraham Maslow left a legacy which included one of today's most often quoted target market research formulas – Maslow's pyramid.

Maslow argued that there are five sets of motivational factors which influence people. As each need intensifies, it evolves into a motive to be fulfilled. Once that motive is satisfied, a person steps up to the next level in the 'pyramid'. Compelling motives further escalate towards the pyramid's pinnacle.

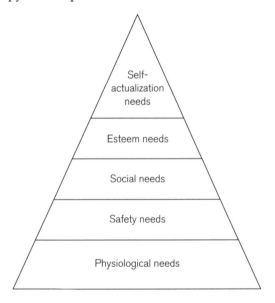

As any marketer can testify, to a great extent, image is everything. In fact, second to power, I regard image as the world's most potent aphrodisiac (especially self-projected image). The market's need to uphold imagery – such as the impressions given to colleagues, family or peers – is tremendous. So using Maslow's pyramid, marketing plans are often devised to help address people's perceptual needs. For example, when selling a pension:

1  *Physiological needs*
   Will a pension pay for food and shelter?

2  *Safety needs*
   Will a pension continue to protect the family's welfare?

3  *Social needs*
   Will a pension maintain membership of a sports or social club?

4  *Esteem needs*
   Will a pension maintain a lifestyle?

5  *Self-development – actualization (fulfilment) needs*
   Will a pensioner later be able to attain what he or she is too busy to achieve currently?

Ironically, hardly anyone ever truly attains level five – self-fulfilment. Maslow discovered that only about 1 per cent of the overall population reach this level, and that typically they were middle-aged or over. Most importantly, they were neurosis free!

Using this hierarchy of needs, if a company were to reinvent a product that could genuinely provide every requirement, the marketing cycle would come to an abrupt halt. After all, people would never again be given a better version of a product or service. So in marketing terms, it pays to keep people wanting more and more through delivering promises with shorter and shorter warranties!

When planning for your own reinvention, consider how each step links with the next. For example:

1  *Physiological needs*
   Will my home be put at risk through reduction of income if I quit the job and start afresh?

2  *Safety needs*
   Will I compromise my position in the pecking order at work if I argue against the traditional way of doing things?

3  *Social needs*
   Will my existing relationships with friends be adversely affected?

4  *Esteem needs*
   Am I happy with how I feel about my current accomplishments – could I feasibly achieve more if I took a reinvention risk?

5  *Self-actualization (fulfilment) needs*
   Upon weighing up the risks and advantages, what is the likelihood that all of my efforts to reinvent myself will have been worthwhile? More importantly, will taking the steps towards reinvention encourage even further adaptations along the line, or will I simply be content to have achieved what I set out to accomplish?

## Three steps to you

Carl Rogers (1902–87) developed a form of psychotherapy called Person Centred Therapy (or Client Centred). He agreed in most parts with Maslow's idea that rather than aiming to reach a specific end goal of self (development) actualization, people repeatedly strive to develop their adeptness to self-actualize (reinvent) themselves. In doing so, they undertake full responsibility for improving (reinventing) their life and circumstances.

Rogers said that people's self-concepts depended on:

1   the ideal self

2   self-image

3   self-esteem.

The smaller the gap between your 'ideal self' and your 'self-esteem',
the higher your perception on how you rate your 'self' both
autonomously and in relation to those around you. Whereas the
bigger the gap between your 'ideal self,' and your 'self-esteem',
the lower your perceptions about how you rate your 'self' as an
autonomous entity and in relation to those around you.

In this way, if you believe that you are at a mid-point in life, you will
only be happy if you earnestly aim at improving your circumstances.
Alternatively, you could address all the issues that have brought you
to your current half-way point, including your emotional luggage.

'No one can make you feel inferior without your consent.'

Eleanor Roosevelt

Either way, you'll probably only find such perceptive degrees of
happiness if you either become totally focused on improving your
circumstances – and so shorten the gap between your 'ideal self'
(where you want to be) and 'self-esteem' – or get on with the
business of addressing the issues, people and circumstances that
have brought you to your current position.

On studying Rogers further, I think that he astutely listed all the
ideal ingredients for a successful reinventor. That is someone who:

1   is open to all experience;

2   is able to live fully in every moment;

3   has the will to follow his or her instincts rather than just the will
    of others;

4   is flexible and when needed spontaneous;

5   is creative.

Sam Goldwyn

Sigmund Freud (1856–1939) the renowned psychiatrist, held an opposing view to that of Maslow. He argued that people don't consciously realize what motivates them. Freud suggested that instead of systematically addressing needs, people repressed cravings, to deal with them on a subconscious level through dreams, slips of the tongue (Freudian slips), neurotically, phobically, obsessively or psychotically. Or to put it simply, whatever you say or do, it inevitably relates back to your relationship with your mother! For example, from Freud's perspective, smoking fulfils a latent desire to suckle at your mother's breast!

Freud divided the psyche into three parts: the id, the ego and the superego.

The *id* represents your instinctive nature and operates by the pleasure principle. It's looking out for the immediate gratification of your senses, with no thought for adverse long-term consequences either for yourself or others. It characterizes the first few years of every human life but lurks in the wings for the remainder.

The *ego* enters human perception around the age of two and operates by the reality principle. The ego is at the centre of a reinventor's cognitive processes. To survive, the ego will occasionally encourage you to make down-to-earth plans for the future. However, by making those plans – especially one's dealing with radical changes – the ego engages with the selfish 'id' head on.

Then there is the *superego*, which arrives on the scene around the age of three. Your superego is like a cross between your guardian angel and a WWF wrestling referee. It's concerned with the ideal side of life, with ethics and your own self-imposed code of conduct. It tries to stop you from being anti-social. It's a bit like Freud's version of Jiminy Cricket, always perched on your shoulder with good advice as a counter-balance to the selfish id.

However, leaving Freud at this point, there is a completely different approach to facing the past and dealing with why you do what you do – that is simply not to think about it! This line of attack is called 'cognitive miserliness'. Everyone has the natural ability to be instinctive. As long as you recognize that you might not understand everything and that one day you may be proven wrong, then providing you have the confidence and self-belief to practise what deep down you feel is right, you may as well go ahead.

As you know, any progress is a one step closer to reinvention and the myriad rewards which it brings.

## REINVENTING YOU

◆ Manage your problems so that you can live life to its full potential.

◆ Pain, if recognized and dealt with, can serve a purpose.

◆ Even after the most dire of circumstances, given time, you can learn to trust again – as long as you have trust in yourself.

◆ If you feel messed up inside, you often look shabby on the outside.

◆ Every problem is important; of equal importance is to put each one into perspective.

◆ Value yourself.

◆ Provided you can keep your cool, any change can be addressed and, in most circumstances, can be turned to advantage.

◆ Remain focused on the here-and-now so that you can enjoy the future.

◆ Delay can be the deadliest form of denial.

◆ When coping with reinvention, trying to reframe your view of the world.

▶

- Your ability to cope with reinvention is often dictated by the example set by those around you.

- Wundt taught that to find answers, you have to look within yourself.

- Often in reinvention, the whole is greater than the parts.

- Consider a step-by-step approach towards reinvention.

- No one can make you feel inferior without your consent.

- Follow your instincts rather than just the will of others.

- Feel free to act occasionally on the spur of the moment.

- Recognize that you don't necessarily have to understand everything, and that one day you may be proven wrong.

- Celebrate your natural talents and exploit them.

- The only truth is what you choose to believe.

- When planning for your reinvention, consider how step-by-step, what you aim for, what complements you really need.

- If you want to present a well-developed image to the outside, start developing your esteem on the inside: you're worth it.

- Your id, ego and superego are all you – it's just a matter of balance – you hold it, so seize the opportunity to be objective.

- Aim to achieve something of substance.

08

# chapter eight
## following beliefs, instincts and choices

reinvent yourself

momentum

Corporations spend hundreds upon thousands of pounds, euros and dollars on company sales, management and marketing training schemes. In the cases of larger organizations (employing over 150 people), a fundamental purpose of training is to teach people to recognize something that subconsciously they knew at the age of one. namely, that they are individuals. As a leader of many of these courses, the oddity of this model never fails to amaze me.

This is especially true in the case of team-building courses and events when companies lull 'worker ants' into believing that through Human Resources schemes like team away-days, group football matches and so on, the ants can discover the concept of communal individuality (CI). You may have heard of this as preached by countless feel-good management and sales gurus wanting your company's training budget.

The concept works like this: to encourage tough workers, push hard team players. Here is how it's delivered in practice.

Workers are encouraged to rejoice in their individuality as promoted by the organization's ethics, e.g. 'Happiness should be your aim'; 'You're an integral part of our priority "numero uno" reinvention project'; 'Be true to yourself through being of service to customers and part of the … [name of organization team].'

Your own staff canteen may be plastered with posters depicting athletes jumping hurdles or mountaineers climbing peaks – all with captions like, 'You can do it' or 'Without you we're nothing, with you, we're everything.'

Next, workers join social gatherings. As with all social gatherings, you invariably come across the odd one or two conflicts of interests and opinions. This is when the principle of CI really sets to work. Leveraging on people's general lack of confidence to confront the issue of conflict, CI draws them to put their differences aside and instead follow the creed of 'acting like a professional'. In short, it gets them back to work as a unit, suppressing personal feelings and replacing them with the quest to ensure that 'the customer must be kept happy': the perfect displacement therapy.

The goal of keeping the customer happy, or at the very least, satisfied, is another aspect of CI. This corporately-endorsed, frequently misrepresented approach to reinvention works best when applied to people working in administration, or on the manufacturing line, or (most typically) as part of a call centre team. In each of these cases, few ever meet customers face-to-face. Most can only gauge customer satisfaction by reports or assumptions. Depending on the authors of such reports as well as instigators of rumours, reported customer satisfaction levels vary wildly.

Believing that team happiness depends on your individual input, and that individual input depends on serving the needs of the all-knowing, all-seeing, all-powerful customer (who is always right) you can often end up paranoid. After all, if the customer isn't kept happy, anything from catastrophic devastation, leading to outright desolation, could befall you and the team, including a plague of complaints and the slaying of the first one in, last one out.

In a desperate act you offer extra overtime, shorter tea and lunch breaks, even shorter loo breaks – a great lesson in corporate bladder control. And just in case you are away from the office, thanks to GPRS telecommunications, you can still be contacted – so even at home – you can remain 'always on'.

It all leads to stress. In an effort to get away from it all, you seek solace from those aforementioned team-led, out-of-hours activities. These bind further your group dynamics and so the story goes on and your real individuality diminishes. You can hold fast to the belief that even if the worst should happen, the company health plan will pay for a month's therapy.

## You are your own vocation

Earlier I explained that your real career is *you*. So is your chosen style of reinvention. You could draw upon your genuine ideas as well as the strength of your convictions to change old processes at work, or tried, tested and botched-up matters at home. You could become a 'reinvention radical', ever ready to change the status quo wherever and whenever you find it. You could emulate the pop stars Bob Geldoff and Bono, showing audacity as well as grit, to shake up some of the world's most traumatic problems.

## Remain true to yourself – but not at the expense of others.

This is your chance – your vocation, your life. Whatever you choose, whichever way you choose to do it, be warned that reinvention doesn't give you the 'green light' to be arrogant and selfish by dismissing everyone else's needs. Following the prophet Job's advice, 'Man was created to learn wisdom', make your first commandment 'Thou shall seek to understand'. It's only through self-improvement and so reinvention – for the good of yourself and not at the cost of others – that everyone can advance.

'One must allow others to be right. It consoles them for not being anything else.'

André Gide

## 'Vaulting ambition which o'erleaps itself …' (*Macbeth*)

Once, during a team-building weekend, my immediate boss outlined how, in order to achieve unlimited promotion, every member of the team should seek to improve themselves with the ultimate unilateral aim of usurping the boss! He elaborated that if every person in the agency were to strive to take over the boss's chair, the agency would go from strength to strength and everyone would prosper. It was inspiring.

As we were packing at the end of the weekend, I decided to take up the challenge. I approached the boss and detailed how I planned to take over his job. Spurred on by the speech, it seemed a golden opportunity to reinvent myself within the agency group. My tactic didn't go to plan: one week later, he sacked me for being too cocky!

It goes to prove that whilst assertion may put you in front, without care and consideration, it can also lead to 'putting your foot in it' and so forcing you to turn your back on greater chances at a later date.

## The American way

I heard a similar story about a salesperson in the United States; the difference was that the boss told him that with sheer determination he would certainly succeed. Within a year the salesperson had become head of the division and eventually ran one of the most successful sales companies of its kind. This is a prime example of a truly successful reinvention, partly because it avoids the famous British style of 'mushroom management', namely, keep everyone in the dark. As any gardener will testify, the trouble with this approach is that as a mushroom is a fungus, you can never be totally sure what shape it will grow into; perhaps something totally unexpected.

The best aspect of the American success story is that through adopting a healthy approach towards the reinvention process, the original boss who motivated the salesperson was in a 'win-win' situation. Not only did he gain from the salesperson's sheer determination, he also enjoyed the personal gratification of mentoring the salesperson's achievements at every opportunity.

## My decision is 'maybe' and that's final

I have led various courses on business assertion. When asking delegates why they attended such events, typical answers were:

'The company felt I wasn't confident enough', 'My boss wants me to speak up at meetings', 'I find it difficult to say "no"'.

It all sounds reasonable. Nevertheless, despite its undoubted importance to employers and their employees, initially the business assertion course was the least booked. Hardly surprising when you consider that for some misguided managers, the purpose of a training course is to teach people how to become products to sell products. Even more aptly, people attend a course to learn techniques to help secure better jobs. The real purpose of training is very different. For example, the purpose of a training course on reinvention would be to help people recognize that contentment starts and ends with themselves and that through humility, it inspires everyone who encounters it en route. (And that's one course that you don't have to pay for – just live it.)

'Every day create your history. Every path you take you're leaving your legacy.'

Michael Jackson

Posters in the staff canteens urge workers to remember maxims as dreamt up by bored copywriters. Typical posters are 'Put the customer first', 'Technology doesn't change lives, people do', or at Acme company: 'People are teams'. The truth is that the most important customer they, or for that matter you, will ever deal with is *you*.

Keep your real 'numero uno' customer happy and you will have the confidence and strength to keep others happy as well. In fact, they will start depending on you to do so. As Victor Frankl, an Auschwitz survivor said, 'Everything can be taken from man but one thing: the last of human freedoms – to choose one's own attitude in any set of circumstances, to choose one's own way.'

## Fight for your rights without defending your wrongs

I teach that business assertion is about upholding your rights, beliefs and opinions. How you assert yourself depends on how you decide to behave under various circumstances, such as having to reinvent your goals.

As an integral part of reinvention, assertion allows you to be honest with yourself and others. It permits you to have the self-confidence to listen to others whilst remaining true to yourself, but not at anyone's expense. Getting what you want on your terms calls for the ability to negotiate in an adult, rational manner. Not everything is fair in love and war, so to reach a workable as well as amicable compromise you need to respect yourself and others.

Lack of assertion leads in many instances to being forced to take on more than you can comfortably handle. Worse still it forces others to match your eagerness, making them feel bad for failing to do as much as you. Ultimately it leads to lower self-esteem because of your high self-expectations. You end up kicking yourself: 'If only I had done or said this or that … I am awful … It's the system's fault …' In the event, everyone suffers: you, the job, family and friends. And that just makes you angry and frustrated.

## Don't get mad – get even

Often the potential harm of anger, including quarrels at work and home, is far greater than the damage that caused the anger in the first place. Aggression is the total opposite of assertion. It's all about getting your own way at someone else's expense. The result is that the people who deal with you simply won't trust you: they feel bruised, undervalued and resentful. In fact, they'll conspire against you and your reinvention schemes, to such an extent, that they'll establish a group of other people who will join in gossiping and tarnishing your reputation.

## Occasionally giving ground can be your greatest form of advancement.

I once watched an episode of *Star Trek* in which crew members, displaying what can only be described as 'bad attitude', were taught that when confronted by aggressive enemy fire from all sides, sometimes the best course of action is not to retaliate with even more missiles. Instead they were trained to retreat. 'After all', explained the ever-logical Vulcan officer, 'The objective of any military strategy is to gain the greatest possible advantage with minimum casualties. Returning aggressive fire would simply have led to being destroyed whilst using up the last of the available ammunition. Besides, it's better to live to fight a war than die fighting a battle.' (This went against the Newton theory which I discussed earlier, yet it certainly caused me to ponder its merits.)

When, in your reinvention process, you come across difficult people, try to keep the conversation flowing. This can be achieved through several cool techniques. The first is to slow them down by asserting what you believe has been said and what you intend to do about it.

For example, dealing with a bullying line-manager:

'You must produce the report by tomorrow – even if it takes all night.'

*'I can appreciate your problem – you feel you need the report by tomorrow.'*

'Well, get on with it.'

*'I can see your problem, I'm sorry but I am busy on other projects.'*

I'm disappointed in you.'

*'As I said, it's not that I don't want to help. I already have other important work so I can't produce the report by tomorrow. However, I could talk to you about it on Friday. Would that help?'*

If that fails, you could always try fogging them – by agreeing in part to what they said – and settle for a compromise.

## Speaking the right language

Power conversations in which you keep on interrupting leads to frustration and a battle of who can get in the last word. Tag conversations are initially less powerful but ultimately more effective. 'Nice coffee – don't you think?'

Reinvention calls for a great deal of 'give' and 'take'. Starting with a tag conversation, you have the opportunity to listen, explain what you think or feel, state your intentions, and finally respond with forecasts. For example, 'If I did "this", then "that" would happen – would that be okay?'

Another response would be to say nothing– until the other person is forced to break the ice – a vital psychological advantage point to you.

So, to recap, listen to what someone is saying, confirm what you hear and how you feel about it, so that you are understood. Then attempt to provide a solution or explain why you believe you can't do it, replaying the original request followed by your answer, bearing in mind that the arguments are usually against a question rather than the person who posed the question. Above all, *respond* to difficult people – never react.

## Assertion confidence model for reinventors

**1** Listen

  **2** Yes, I understand

    **3** Explain

      **4** Instant replay

        **5** No (A 'no' a day keeps the aggravations away – and the ulcers too!)

Have faith and passion in what you feel so that you can never be accused of being a fraud. (People may disagree with you but nobody can ever take away what you feel.) Never accept that you are cornered into doing something you don't want to do, unless by acceding you will be gaining. Stick to what you believe in and let others see that you are a rock in unsteady waters and so can be trusted.

Be prepared too to accept help and be willing to help others to achieve what you believe in for the good and benefit of everyone concerned (another vital aspect of reinvention). Know when to be seen to do something with conviction and when to stop yourself from doing something that you may regret later.

## Re-program your head

During the late 1990s there was a great call for training courses, motivational seminars and books about NLP: that is , 'Neuro', representing the mind and how it is used to organize a person's thinking; 'Linguistic', how to use language and the effects of doing so, and 'Programming', dealing with sequences of repetitive behaviour and acting with purpose. Connecting all three aspects, NLP is about learning how to program neurology and language to achieve positive results.

It was started jointly by Richard Bandler and John Grinder, who were looking for a way to help people change by teaching them to program their brains. In adopting NLP, adherents could reach their full potential. As such, NLP can be likened to a reinventor's manual to his or her mind. As Richard Bandler said,

**The more you want to become creative, the more you have not only to elicit other people's strategies and replicate them yourself, but also modify others' strategies and have a strategy that brings about new creativity strategies based on as many wonderful states as you can design for yourself.**

In replicating others' strategies and even idiosyncrasies, some say that NLP teaches you what people are thinking and feeling – simply by watching for non-verbal clues expressed through body language. The best place to look for such clues in this theatre of language is the face, which can express six fundamental feelings and emotions:

- anger

- fear

- happiness

- sadness

- surprise

- disgust.

Of course, none of these emotions can be fully taken at face 'value'. You can, for example, feel happy as well as surprised.

Body language communications could include actions such as people scratching their nose, which may mean that they are lying. Holding palms upwards means 'implore', whereas as palms forward means 'repel' and inwards, 'embrace'. The danger is that it can become too easy to take other people's actions out of context. For example, shaking one's head is more often than not interpreted as a negative gesture. However, 'no' in Greece is an upward head toss. In the United States making a circle by holding the first finger against the thumb means OK, whereas in southern France it signifies being worthless, in the Middle East it is an obscenity, while in Japan it stands for money.

To some, at best, NLP can teach potential reinventors some fascinating truths about themselves and their relationships with those whom they wish to emulate. At worst, it can be compared with a gypsy fortune-teller at the local carnival.

## Gestures or jesters?

- Hands clasped together means you feel uneasy or controlled.

- Blocking the mouth with hands: you are lying or stopping yourself from saying something wrong.

- Crossing your arms or legs: you are unconvinced or 'switched off' to any ideas.

- Leaning forward: you are ready for action and eager to learn.

- Leaning backwards: you are confident, or you've 'heard it all before'.

- Picking the lint off your clothes whilst others are talking: you disapprove of what you hearing.

- Thumbs sticking out of your jacket pockets: you are taking charge of a situation.

- Arms held out whilst standing: you are open, sincere and have nothing to hide.

- Leaning across a table whilst standing up: you believe that you are in charge.

NLP explains that:

- 7 per cent of human communication is through words. People often tend to interpret words as they think fit, rather than what is actually being said.

- 38 per cent of human communication relates to your tone of voice, accent and nuance. This enables listeners to decide what parts should receive the greatest attention.

- 55 per cent of communication deals with body talk – in other words, your posture and breathing patterns. How you appear and act – from what you wear, to how your body language supports your mood – are the most important aspects of communication.

## Getting to grips

How you deal with a given situation boils down to controlling your own neural system or state of mind. Although we share the same basic nervous system, many don't use it to its full potential. This is highlighted when you hear someone who has just read an article about NLP say something like, 'Hey guys, did you know that I only use 10 per cent of my brain power!' That's like saying, 'Hey guys, did you know that apparently I have the mental capacity to achieve more, but I am just too stupid to do anything about it!'

# Get on other people's wavelength – but tune into yours.

Through NLP or just common sense you can nurture your talents by aligning your reinvention needs to other people's values. It's a bit like playing jazz. You hear the score that you admire and then you move it up tempo or if you prefer, down tempo. You skip sections that are too dull and linger on others that are more in tune with your playing. In the end, you have an improvised piece of music that features the right mix of rhythm along with a touch of soul, rock 'n roll, house, blues and most of all – *you*.

So, if in your quest for reinvention, you admire a person's drive to make money, you could study the patterns that they follow, and see if you could do likewise. If you admire how such a person always finds time to be with the family, you could also study how they manage a busy schedule whilst still being highly regarded at work.

You often find that successful people are enthusiastic about what they do and how they express it. In your state of reinvention, ask yourself if you also share such a passion or could become passionate about a particular subject.

You may find that successful people have distinctive beliefs – what do *you* believe in and why?

You may find that successful people follow a set strategy. Devise your own set of questions to help realize your ambitions. Follow them through from the planning stage, to implementation and final result.

## Planning and goals

◆ Do you consistently stretch targets yet understand limitations?

◆ Do you share the same values of the people who seem to get what they want? Are your values balanced?

◆ Do you actually want to be a success and can you visualize your reinvented success, not just in the distant future but in the foreseeable one as well?

- Picturing that success, what do you imagine will happen to your life, and the lives of the key people around you, once you have become successful?

- What is stopping you from shaping those goals right now?

- Do you ensure that everyone around you understands your objectives, however often revised?

- Do you attract allies to support your reinvention project?

- Can you convert 'non-believers' into advocates for reinvention?

- Do you believe in change with a tangibly beneficial aim in mind, rather than for its own sake?

- Do you expect from others what you could achieve for yourself?

- Do you strive to ensure that reinvention has the potential for even greater benefits and more valuable change?

- Are you proud to reinvent yourself?

## Implementation

- Do you allow yourself and others a reasonable timescale to implement a reinvention project?

- Are you willing to implement reinvention in stages, rather than in one go?

- In your personal and professional life, do you emulate the exemplary behaviour of others?

- Can you be depended upon to offer a shoulder to lean on when needed?

- Do you make people feel good about themselves?

- Do you have a high energy level – perhaps like the people who generally seem to be always 'on the ball'? (Perhaps you need to look at your diet and exercise programme. *See* 'Fit Defence'.)

- Do you discuss your ideas with friends and colleagues before going ahead with them?

## Results

- Do you believe that by helping others you reinforce ties with colleagues, family and friends?

- Do you listen to yourself as well as to others?

- Do you reward yourself and others for achievements?

- Can you be pragmatic with humility when it comes to asking others to change or consider changing?

- Do you thank people for their time and efforts in helping you succeed?

- Following the advice to be like a postage stamp (i.e. stick to one thing until you get there), can you complete existing projects to the best of your ability before starting new ones?

- Does making others feel good about themselves improve your own self-esteem?

- Do you believe that although people may fall along their route towards reinvention, what really matters is how fast they can get back up on their feet?

- Are you really open to suggestions or just claim superficially to be so?

- Do you believe that when you find someone special, anything is possible – especially if that someone is *you*?

- Can you measure success in yourself and others?

- Is that success measured by peace of mind?

- Are you the kind of person that could be a role model for young people?

- Do you make strong, positive impressions on others when you meet them through techniques such as establishing eye contact and using expressive, but controlled body gestures?

- Does what you wear reflect how you feel whilst making those around also feel comfortable? (*See* 'Perceptions and Misconceptions'.)

Do you come across as:

◆ Competent?

◆ Confident?

◆ Credible?

◆ Consistent in your message?

◆ Controlled in how you pace that message?

## The uniformity of mediocrity

When replicating other people's values, avoid what I call the 'frequent business traveller's hotel syndrome'. This is when you find that every hotel you stay at looks the same – whatever the country; whatever the continent – even down to the bathroom layout.

'Plus ça change, plus c'est la même chose.'
('The more things change, the more they stay the same.')

Alphonse Carr

If you go too far trying to replicate or integrate other people's ideas into your own, you could end up replicating mediocrity; one of the scourges of modern-day living.

Once you have devised your *own* set of values, beliefs and action patterns, it's up to you to stick to them. That takes discipline as well as skill in pinpointing what you want for the right 'positive' reasons. For although you may have discovered a strategy for change, you still have to be consistent in your pursuit of reinvention.

As with any strategic project, in terms of making the right kind of choice, it's your call. The greatest choice is to want to be different – not for difference's sake but for your own. For example, if a company that wishes to reinvent itself only benchmarks their goals against competitors, it will end up achieving the same as everyone else. In such cases, true reinvention tactics – like being *distinctive* through understanding how strengths can be stretched to meet everyone's satisfaction, including employees, suppliers and ultimately customers – get thrown out of the window.

Even if you have identified characteristics in others that you would want for yourself, you still don't have to commit yourself totally to those traits. Instead, try the hunt-and-peck method to choose what suits you best. In other words, look for what you admire, peck off what you can chew, digest what you like, and ignore the rest.

## How to engineer a wobble

In engineering there is a fundamental called 'The Square Law of Computation'. It states that for every component of a system – for every extra equation in a problem – the amount of computation required to solve the system increases at least as quickly as the square of the number of equations. Or to put it in 'everyday' terms: if the intricacy of your problem doubles, the time it takes to solve it quadruples. The way around this is to simplify your problem by concentrating on core issues.

For example, astronomers are always searching for new stars. However, there are billions of stars in the Solar System, each exerting a gravitational pull on others. To find new 'invisible' stars, astronomers have to spot 'wobbles' around the stars generated by the gravitational pulls from nearby 'visible' stars. In so doing astronomers tend to ignore most of the other objects in outer space. In short they choose which aspects of the Solar System to concentrate upon, rather than being overwhelmed by the sheer vastness of the universe and being led off-course by too many wobbles!

In your approach to handling what can first appear as an Everest-size problem, remember that you don't always have to take on the whole world to resolve one or two core issues.

## You don't need to boil an ocean to get a handful of salt.

# Stay focused

Sometimes the allure of reinvention is so seductive that the sheer scale of its potential can overwhelm you. This is when you need to remind yourself about the importance of remaining focused and the futility of aiming to make such radically irreversible changes to your life. Without such precaution, you could end up in a worse state than when you started.

This is commonplace with people who take reinvention to the point of a surgeon's knife, and are prepared to undergo plastic surgery. If only it were all as simple as nipping off bits and pieces of stuff you didn't like, and adding on bits you would prefer! In terms of reinvention, the deepest cuts aren't necessarily the sharpest ones. Concentrate on the issues that are bothering you from *within* and you'll change the way they appear from *without*.

If I keep saying to myself 'I can't lose weight', I probably won't. Similarly, if you tell children that they can't watch television, they probably will reach for the remote control in defiance. Why? The mind 'zeros-in' on the issue that most preoccupies it. If left to its own devices, syntax like 'can't and 'can' goes out of the window.

Through understanding and focusing on your goals and weaknesses, you can break down a sentence like ' I don't have time to exercise' into the key elements of 'time' and 'exercise'. 'Time' is important because of your perceived lack of it, and 'exercise' because of your perceived struggle against it. Now you can recognize the things that bother you and commit yourself to doing something about it – turn the negative *'don't'* into a positive *'do'*.

You may think, 'That's okay for you to say. I still have to face the dread of doing the exercise at the expense of my time, which is precious.' That's a typical reaction by people who don't really want or care to reinvent. It's not that they don't accept that a change can be to their benefit; it's that they are not prepared to act on instincts. In other words, like most of us, they fear failure. As I mentioned earlier in this book, fear can slow or even halt your true ability to get what you want. Perhaps it's because you are afraid of the consequences of what will happen once you take action.

Of course, if you don't act within the practical limits of your own capability, you'll still get a consequence from your action. Unfortunately, it may not be what you ideally hoped for, but what you – and you alone – deserve. The more decisions you make, the better your decision-making skills become.

## Define your fate

In life, everything you do has a consequence. Some of the results may not be to your liking. But that doesn't mean the end of your quest to change issues and events.

*The Oxford English Dictionary* defines the word 'consequence' as 'a result or effect of an action or condition'. Several hundred pages on, it lists another word 'subsequence', defined as 'the state of following something, especially as a result or effect'. So just as subsequence follows consequence, depending on how you deal with a given situation, you always get another chance to start afresh and, who knows, may end up producing a better result than the one originally planned.

Your past experience contributed to your final choice. On the other hand, if you decide to leave everything in the hands of fate, or to be more precise, in the hands of people with the confidence to shape destiny – theirs or yours – then in effect you are discarding your own ability to shape the consequences of your actions. You become powerless and those other people affecting your life virtually take over.

## I may be dying to succeed, but I'm not going to kill myself over it.

Ambition shouldn't mean working yourself to death so that you can live better. Working life can sometimes seem like a rat race. With a little planning you can turn *RAT RACE* into the *ART* of *CARE* – for your own good.

Treat your reinvention plans in terms of a figure of speech called a *chiasmus*. For example: 'Never let a fool kiss you or a kiss fool you'. 'A statesman is a politician who places himself at the service of the nation. A politician is a statesman who places the nation at his service.' In other words, 'one should reinvent to live, not live to reinvent'.

When I was commissioned to write this book, I was frightened of the consequences. Did I really have the ability to write such a deeply thought out work? It was a challenge. Had I declined, I would have affirmed any latent beliefs – warranted or otherwise – that I couldn't achieve any more in my writing career.

As I enter the final stages of the book, I feel great. In fact, completion of any worthwhile project always gives a real 'buzz' of satisfaction. Once you have completed your own initial reinvention project, people will know that you are a person who perseveres. Perseverance usually means trust, and trust leads to self-confidence.

'Some men see things as they are and say "why?" I dream things that never were and say "why not?" '

John F. Kennedy

You too can question your fear of consequences:

'I can't do it.'
   *Who's stopping you?*

'She thinks I'm stupid.'
   *Have you asked her?*

'Life is dull.'
   *Whose life is it anyway?*

'Everything bad that happens to me is everyone else's fault.'

*You'll only change external events by starting to reinvent what's going on within yourself.*

'Reinvention is too difficult.'
   *How difficult/easy do you want to make it?*

'I have a bad attitude at work and at home because my life is dreadful.'
   *Hey buddy – have you checked out your bad attitude lately?*

'I've always been a good person and done my best. Now everything has turned against me. So I've come to the conclusion that any ideological purposes such as to improve and reinvent my work, home, social or even religious beliefs that I may have once held, are worthless.'
   *If you only ever do things for a reward, you are in for a big disappointment. On the other hand, if you do something simply for its own sake, the reward is the act of doing it!*

'Why do bad things always happen to me?'
   *Who put you in that position?*

'I might look confident at my job, but deep down I have absolutely no idea about what I am doing.'
   *Maybe you stopped listening to what you really needed and instead concentrated too much on what you felt you ought to have.*

'I can't turn to anyone for support.'
   *Have you looked at yourself in the mirror lately?*

'I ought to do something about my life.'
   *Don't just think – act on your instincts!*

'My boss will never really give me a chance to improve myself.'
   *Have you asked for a chance, and having asked, questioned yourself why you weren't given one?*

'I'll never find enough hours in the day to get everything done in time.'
   *Are you spending too much time looking at the clock and not enough at the projects in hand?*

'I am a total workaholic – I have to be, what with the ever-looming threat of redundancies. So I am always working on projects – that's the crux of the problem!'

*Have you made the occasional 'just doing nothing' one of your key projects?*

'Life is a gravely serious matter. I take my job and myself too seriously.'

*Remind yourself of the sheer delight from just fooling around for the sake of it. Have fun! After all, what's the point of stress if it gives you varicose brains?*

'People only care about anything if it's in their own interest to do so.'

*Being realistic, I probably can't deny this, so make it in your interest to reinvent yourself – for your own sake!*

## Remoulding the future

In 1949, the American National Bureau of Standards invented a type of black gooey substance that promised to break the normal laws of physics on demand. It was called Convertible Goop. Embedded in the substance were micrometre-sized iron particles. When a magnetic force was applied, the north pole in one iron particle attracted the south pole in another. The result was that the goo became a solid. It was an amazing, but at the time, pretty redundant discovery.

Fifty years on, the automobile industry recalled the discovery and decided to incorporate the substance into shock absorbers.

An important lesson to learn from this is that through widening your potential, even moderately, each day you learn something new about yourself. That knowledge is forever developing. Its fruits may not become immediately apparent. However, one day (you can never be sure when) that knowledge will be ripe for picking and perfect for putting into practice.

Providing you keep to your own set of beliefs and values, you too can stretch beyond what most people would ever dare to reach, in the knowledge that you can always return to your core values and strengths.

## Become a devotee of reinvention

Ethics play a vital role in reinvention. However, there's little point in *praying* on your knees at the weekend if you spend the rest of the week *preying* on your acquaintances.

I asked the Chief Rabbi of the United Kingdom for his views. 'Re-inventing yourself', he said, 'is called in Judaism *teshuvah*, a difficult word to translate. It means "repentance", "return", "coming back" to the person you ought to be and were meant to be.'

I then asked him how to go about achieving this. Extracts from the discussion are set out below:

There are two stages. First, hear the call; second, learn how to heed it. The first is to learn how to listen. This is one of the hardest arts in the world. You have to be able to filter out criticism based on envy, rivalry, sheer bloody-mindedness etc. and hear the still, small voice of truth beneath the noise. Have friends who'll be honest and whom you know seek your good. Constantly reflect on what you were put on this earth to do …

I have a principle that has served me well for many years. It goes: 'Don't do what you do well. Do what only you can do.' Many people fail to be what they could become because they do many things well, while ignoring what only they can do (what Milton called, 'that one talent. Which is death to hide'). Constantly reflect – as impersonally as possible – on what needs to be done. If you can match vocation and need – what only you can do and what objectively needs to be done – you have discovered your private heaven to survive any hell.

The second – the actual reinvention – goes like this. In the immortal words of the Nike advertisement, 'Just do it'. Once you've thought hard, beware lest 'the native hue of resolution is sicklied o'er by the pale cast of thought'. If you can't just do it, put yourself in a situation where you cannot afford to fail. External necessity can be more powerful than the strongest willpower. It can draw from us a reservoir of strength we didn't know we possessed.

Get friends to help you. It took me 20 years to write my first book. Eventually I got some people close to me to enquire, ' what about the next book?' From then on, it was easy: over the past 12 years, I've written 14 books ...

Defeat your own tendency to defeat yourself. Know what it takes to help other people help you (and if you don't know, still ask them). Always guard against a situation (technically it's called co-dependency) in which you are sabotaging their efforts to help you change.

Surround yourself with people who are strong in areas where you are weak. Empower them, praise them and never forget that you can achieve anything you want so long as you don't mind who gets the credit ...

Never lose sight of where you want to be. Put it on the first page of your Filofax; read it first thing in the morning. Remember, 100 failures don't add up to a single defeat unless you decide to make it so. Learn to take risks. Treat every failure as a learning experience. Know that every failure is a necessary step on the path to success. I keep a 'good news file' and read it whenever I feel down ...

Never ever seek to be popular. Instead, earn the respect of people you respect. And always remember – to grow is to be alive. Once you stop growing, you start dying. Do all these things for long enough and, I promise, you'll get there.


## Tests and tribulations

To be balanced, I asked Sahib Mustaqim Bleher from the Islamic Party of Great Britain for his views.

Islam subscribes to ongoing personal development. Life on earth from an Islamic perspective is seen as an arena of tests and tribulations which need to be responded to, at times by fighting and standing up to situations. At other times, perseverance and patience, known as *sabr*, will be the appropriate response until matters improve. Very much like grass bending in the wind – waiting to rise again, whereas being rigid like a twig would result in being broken or damaged. When neither option will do there is *hijrah* or migration, moving away from a harmful place or situation and starting all over again elsewhere.

Whereas the loss of human decision making is the result of having to respond to events outside our control, Islam places great emphasis on planning and regular corrections for drift. The path through life is described as the straight path, and to stay on it one must continually reassess one's direction and return to it after any deviations.

A Muslim is meant to be ambitious. When it comes to reinventing, Islam sits uneasily with the notion of man as the master of his own fate: rather than reinventing, the Muslim tries to remodel himself/herself again and again vis-à-vis the example of other humans – prophets or saints – whom God had permitted to excel in their mastery of the challenges posed by living on earth.

## 'Walk humbly' – Book of Micah, chapter VI, verse 8

My brother Raphael is a businessman who travels the world. As a religious Jew, he wears a *kippa* (skullcap). Donning such headgear is a form of committed responsibility accepting that wherever he travels, people will recognize him as a Jew. In being so recognized, he is fully aware that his moral, social and professional performance reflects on Judaism worldwide. It is similar for devoted followers of other religions such as Islam, Christianity and many more who wear items such as a Habit, Hijab, Kufi, Turban or Smagh.

What if you wore a visible sign that identified your positive values to the world? Imagine, for example, if one of the world's most upbeat brand emblems – the dynamic tick belonging to Nike – symbolized your commitment towards being realistically constructive, towards yourself and others. Would you continue to act as you do today? Would you act as if every event in your life had a purpose and that the greatest event of all – your life – along with its ups and downs, became your greatest purpose of all? Would you commit yourself to changes at any cost but at no harm to yourself and others? Would you be the kind of person that others would want to emulate, a leader who recognizes people's beliefs and values and is willing to share your own?

Would you, could you – *do you?*

- Follow your own book of principles.

- Your career is you.

- Encourage others to improve themselves.

- Contentment starts with you; through humility, it inspires everyone who encounters it en route.

- Make your number one customer *you*.

- You have the right to your own opinions.

- Remain true to yourself, but not at the expense of others.

- Have self-respect and respect for others.

- Don't mistake assertion for aggression.

- Use assertion to get your point across.

- Listen to what you are told, confirm what you hear and feel about it, and then explain your beliefs.

- Respond to difficult people – don't react.

- A firm 'NO' a day keeps the ulcers away.

- Have faith and passion in what you feel.

- Don't be cornered into doing what you don't want to do.

- Accept help when it is offered.

- Stop doing what you may regret later.

- Don't read too much into people's body language. However, recognize the basic signs.

- Seven per cent of communication is via words.

- Thirty-eight per cent relates to your tone of voice.

- Fifty-five per cent is down to 'body talk'.

- Make 100 per cent count – and that's down to you.

- Allow reinvention to dance to *your* kind of music.

- Never copy mediocrity.

- Devise your own set of values, beliefs and action patterns.

- Be consistent in your pursuit of reinvention.

- Don't be different for difference's sake, do it for yours.

- Aim to be distinctive rather than divisive.

- Concentrate on the core issues that mean the most to your happiness and ignore the rest. The rest tend to fall into place.

- Recognize the things that bother you and deal with them.

- Everything you do has a consequence, so do the right thing.

- To gain power, take control.

- Interpretation is subjective. Try to be objective about reinvention and its implementation.

- Stretch beyond what others wouldn't dare to reach.

- Once you stop growing, you start dying.

- Your life is your greatest purpose.

# chapter nine
## rebranding you

Increasingly, your world is defined by the brands that you consume. For example, I choose to work on an Apple Mac computer. Its brand suggests that I 'think different'. Many others also prefer Apple because its brand campaign intimates that it has reinvented computer hardware from being an office necessity into becoming an essential fashion fixture.

Brands originated from American cowboys who 'branded' their cattle for identification purposes. In our global economy where people and companies compete for recognition, it has become clear that great brands are not reaffirmed simply by general recognition of logos. To endure, a brand has to be based upon a definitive set of identifiable values. Those values have to be consistent wherever and however they are presented. Similarly, conveying your reinvention image isn't purely a matter of wearing the right clothes to match your style and mood. What is more important is how you act and your consistency in realizing genuine personal beliefs.

Depending on how you represent those beliefs – through your deeds rather than declaration of intent – the people with whom you associate will either admire, ignore or, if you get personal branding and reinvention really wrong, conspire against you and follow instead someone else's ideals.

In terms of resemblance, reinvention and rebranding are 'first cousins'. Both engender reputations influenced by clear abilities to deliver what is promised by their campaigns. That's why both need to be based on substance rather than hype.

# It's the real thing …

One of the greatest attractions of a brand is its promise to be 'the genuine article'. In other words, not a copycat or 'look-alike'. Your reinvention process too needs to be based on authentic beliefs rather than 'me-too' facsimiles.

Once people trust your legitimacy, they come also to believe in your potential. This is because, in their search for sincerity, the majority of people want to believe that someone, somewhere can be trusted to push social, political and economic boundaries forward for the greater benefit all-round. If *you* appear to be that person, follow-on support will be assured.

To be considered as a person who pushes the boundaries of convention rather than settles to survive within fences of mediocrity, you need to have absolute confidence in reliability. In other words, you have to reinvent yourself into the sort of person that can be called upon when people need someone to stand up for something worth believing in.

Many brands encourage people to rebel against traditions, including ageing wisdom as depicted by other more established brands. In this way, new brands can establish their own foothold in a market. Everyone likes to feel rebellious in some way or another. It's part of the make-up which encourages us all to assert individuality. Providing your reinvention plan reinforces those feelings, you are bound to succeed.

# Simply the best

A further convergence of reinvention and branding is an aspiration to be associated with 'the best'. For example, wearing what is at least perceived to be 'the best' fashion accessories, or eating at 'the best' restaurants and staying at 'the best' hotels. This type of brand association helps people place themselves in a social pecking order.

In terms of reinvention, this type of social status can be likened to belonging to a circle of influencers who wield sufficient power and sway to promote further your reinvention ideals. (*See* 'Great to See You Again'.)

# May the brand be with you.

Powerful brands motivate people to recognize their full potential. Often the brand serves to reassure people that such potential, however latent, can be brought to the surface simply by displaying the brand. Similarly as a reinventor, you can adopt a policy of empowerment through drawing out what you truly believe and then presenting it, on your own terms, to the world. This reminds me of the most famous premise of the French philosopher, Descartes: 'I think therefore I am'. In terms of brand and reinvention empowerment, *you are, therefore, you do.*

## Welcome to reinvention land

Today's consumer appetites for brands are so voracious that brands need to be realized through as many media and means as possible. This includes what is called 'living a brand experience'. Such experiences are often depicted by websites promoting brand ideals and philosophies, rather than just material products and services. Experiences can also manifest themselves through recreational and work places such as Disneyland and 'trendy' office environments.

As a reinventor, you may interpret 'living a brand experience' as the way you assimilate your values into everyday contact with the people who matter most. In other words, don't just practise what you preach. Assuming your values to be mutually advantageous, ensure that your practice becomes an integral part in the life of the person who so chooses to adopt it.

# If 'necessity is the mother of invention', meet dad = guilt

In over two decades of working in advertising and marketing, I have learnt that guilt remains one of the key motives for people to buy a product or service. Often people invest long-term in brands because peer pressure obliges them to do so. (Choosing a brand is certainly not just a one-off buying opportunity. It's more a continued investment in both time and money.) There may be peer pressure to buy a certain brand of motorbike because of its image, or pressure to eat a certain brand of food because of its health connotations. For the accomplished reinventor, guilt can also prove to be a potent weapon. For sure, people may wish to ignore your reinvention, but if they do, they may be doing a great injustice to both you and the participating community affected by your ambition to improve issues.

Most of all, great brands are universally understood and appreciated across all ages and demographics. Equally, in order to ensure the broad acceptance of your reinvention, the values upon which it is based should be ingeniously simple and unpretentiously inspired.

## Advice from the top

I asked Jamie Dow, a consumer psychologist whose company, The Brand Development Centre Ltd, advises some of the world's leading companies, for his views on reinvention and branding.

**Q** *Why do people and brands reinvent themselves?*

Society is in a constant state of flux, so we modify our behaviour accordingly. The ubiquitous and omnipresent nature of social fluidity means that change in the world around us is sometimes imperceptible. It takes place without our noticing because it slips 'under the radar'.

By way of analogy, parents who are with their children on a more or less ever-present basis don't notice day-to-day changes in the children's physiological development. A godparent who only sees the child on a birthday may say 'How you've grown!'

There are parallels within reinvention and marketing. For example, Heinz regularly changes its corporate identity (that is, the way it physically presents its brand name on the can) – in fact, so regularly that the consumer doesn't realize that it's happened. Regularly changing the packaging's visual means that they only have to make slight adjustments each time. It's as though the brand [the set of associations, values or expectations which accompany the name] has an in-built thermostat. Heinz puts the setting to 'contemporary' and the marketing infrastructure does the rest, marginally tweaking this or that element by a degree here and an iota there as and when required.

People too constantly reinvent themselves. Humans have their own integral antennae which help decipher what is and isn't appropriate behaviour in a given situation.

Because we're on automatic pilot much of the time, the way in which we present ourselves to the world often takes place at the subconscious level. For example, many tend to have a set routine before going to bed and again upon waking up. Rituals such as drawing the curtains and then taking your watch off before settling in for the night, sometimes only become apparent when one of the elements is missing.

Tactile receptors tell the brain that there is something missing from the psychological landscape. To many, the English FA cup without Manchester United isn't the FA cup. For the immediate future at least, the Manhattan skyline ceased to be the Manhattan skyline after 11 September 2001.

Again, there are parallels in marketing. Why didn't packet cake mixes take off on Day One? Why didn't washing powders with built-in conditioners take off at all?

In the case of packets of instant cake mixes, the manufacturer of Viota cakes responded to a slump in sales by adding to the instructions: 'Then add an egg'. Whilst the housewife had previously appreciated the convenience of the product, this rational benefit had been outweighed by the guilt of not having played much of a part in 'making' the cake. The relative inconvenience of adding an extra step to the preparation process when the product was re-launched was outweighed by the emotional gratification the housewife felt having metaphorically given something of herself in the process.

In the case of washing powder, Procter & Gamble no doubt expected their washing powder Bold 3 to be a winner. It wasn't. An emotional ingredient was missing from the product-usage element of the brand experience.

# The housewife felt she allegorically added love when she poured in a liquid fabric conditioner.

Moreover, the fact that her washing machine had a compartment specifically designed for the liquid acted as a guilty reminder each and every time she opened the compartment to add Bold 3.

When concentrated detergents were introduced, some consumers persisted with using the same amount they'd always used. Initially, manufacturers were delighted because the consumer's rate of purchase increased.

In exchange for the convenience, marketing departments believed the consumer would happily pay a premium price for a concentrated detergent. The concentrated bottle was smaller and therefore took up less space in both the shopping basket and the cupboard. However, the consumers complained that they still had to go shopping just as frequently as ever and the concentrated detergent didn't last any longer than the original powder. Besides which, they still loathed the idea of shopping for everyday household products.

Gradually, manufacturers and consumers went through a joint learning curve. The former introduced larger formats and the latter used less in each wash. Both were happy.

**Q** *Do you think that people are their own brands?*

If defined as a distinctive set of expectations that are associated with a name, everyone is potentially a brand. It's what is often described as someone's 'character'. Unfortunately, the word's been overused of late. I think people mistake it for 'resilience'.

I mention 'character' in connection with people as brands because the phrase 'behaving out of character' immediately comes to mind. The existence of such semiotic constructs shows that we do think of people as brands.

From an individual's perspective there is an expectation that a certain brand will behave in a certain way, i.e. 'in character'. Similarly, we have expectations, in the form of stereotypes, about how people behave at the individual or group level. These have been deemed non-politically correct of late because they are discriminatory. Sorry, but stereotypes tend to be accurate. Their disrepute is the result of people misunderstanding or, in some cases, deliberately misinterpreting, what is a stereotype.

A stereotype is one of the many linguistic and cognitive tools that we use to manage data or signals. It's a way of managing sensory overload.

The people in charge of the British Metropolitan Police recently received bad publicity for saying that most muggers are black. However harsh that sounds, the fact remains that from the figures I have seen, most muggers happen to be black [although this ignores many other complex factors behind the figures. –Ed.]. This is not the same of course as saying that all black people are muggers. It's also a fact that most victims of mugging are black.

It isn't only police personnel who are culprits in the misuse of language. The people responsible for managing brands, rather than reinventing them, can be just as guilty. They often refer to 'the brand' when they mean the product or service that underlies it, its name or the company that makes it. Moreover, sometimes brand managers don't even understand the true sense of what is a brand. It is the essence, meaning, gestalt or DNA of what the consumer feels or experiences at an emotional level when interfacing with the brand.

Tellingly, marketing professionals find words such as 'personality' and 'character' are the most helpful in describing the values or expectations that a given brand represents.

In other words, the concept that underlies brands is borrowed from the world of people, rather than people borrowing branding from the world of product and service marketing.

Both the consumer and the company invest in a brand and so both expect a return. However, their respective definitions of what constitutes value differ. The company adopts the accountancy criterion of return on investment (ROI) and measures it in financial terms, namely sales and profitability. The consumer, on the other hand, assesses the brand in terms of the totality of the experience: Does the product or service itself fulfil its role at a functional level and overall, and how does the consumer react as a result of being associated with it?

You may have bought a hi-fi that performs in the way you need, and expected, but if you find a competitor offering the same for less, or that the new advertising for your hi-fi makes you cringe or maybe even angry, then you'll re-assess not only your feelings towards the brand but also always whether to buy one of its products again.

**Q** Why do companies reinvent themselves?

When most people hear 'Geest', they immediately say 'Bananas'. In fact, that's just about the only foodstuff that the brand is not involved with nowadays! Geest is major player across the complete range of fresh fruit and veg and make even more profits from supplying the likes of Marks and Spencer, Sainsbury and Tesco with prepared foodstuffs, including ethnic ready-meals. So, yes, they have no bananas!

Companies need to portray their brands in a way that is relevant to the market. They can point to Virgin as an example of diversification. Virgin may counterpoint that they could diversify because they were a brand, i.e. actually stood for something which people wanted to identify with. At another level, there's reinventing the name and/or how it is presented.

All too often, companies reinvent themselves as a knee-jerk reaction. Like the concept of Customer Relationship Management (CRM) and Customer Loyalty programmes that preceded it, reinvention has become fashionable.

Companies should dig deep into the consumer psyche to identify latent demand and rigorously interrogate their product or service to find a matching benefit before encapsulating it in the brand.

# A reinvented brand should permeate the entire stick of rock, not simply constitute its sugary coating.

**Q** *How about that saying – a leopard can't change its spots?*

A leopard is a biological fact. A brand is a conceptual entity. You can therefore change what it stands for. It should be an evolutionary rather than revolutionary process. As Mao Tse-Tung said, 'A journey of a thousand miles begins with one step.'

Products and services have a finite lifespan. Brands only die through mismanagement of their metamorphosis or marketing 'murder'. Companies need realistic sets of expectations for the brand. Much the same can be said of people seeking to reinvent themselves. You can slowly bring out the various weapons in your armoury of personal assets in response to what those around you are looking for. It's a question of knowing which to pull out when and how to use it to maximum effect.

**Q** *What about people who urge reinventors to be happy with their lot?*

There's a lot to be said for the idea of 'Learning to Love Yourself'. Buddhists have found an inner peace because they have a perception of what they see as the master-plan and a view on their role within it.

Brands need to fully understand what people's hope and fears are if they are to fulfil their true potential. It's important to identify which of these they need the most help with. The next stage is to speculate what the nature of a brand offers. Only then should you start to worry about how to communicate it.

Just as brands need to break out of the stranglehold of passivity, so people must realize that it's not just what the world does to them but also what *they* do to the world. It is perhaps no coincidence that a major study of 1,000 successful women in the United States, published a couple of years ago, found that self-belief was their most dominant distinguishing trait.

Stepping on a banana skin is less problematic if you've got a strategy or a set of goals.

Companies seeking to reinvent themselves should concentrate on satisfying existing customers and translating that satisfaction into loyalty. In conclusion, markets are fragmented into so many niches these days that it's not feasible to stray too far from a brand's hinterland.

## Measuring up your reinvention

Let me further strengthen Jamie's expertise: In measuring the effectiveness of your personal reinvention/re-branding, you could use a brand assessment technique which is similar to the kind practised by many of the world's leading brand consultancies. Let us look at each of the elements that should be measured in such an assessment: brand extent; brand sway; brand magnitude; brand affinity; brand sensitivity.

### Brand extent

This is how well an established brand works in areas beyond its original core market, without compromising the brand's initial set of values.

From your reinvention stance, this equates with your ability to 'fit in' with people beyond your inner circle of friends and acquaintances. Providing that through reaching beyond what is familiar, you don't compromise your core beliefs.

### Brand sway

This can be defined as the commitment given by people within various markets, including the internal market (employees and shareholders). In other words, it's how they feel towards a brand.

In personal reinvention terms, whether you have found that your wider circle of acquaintances as well as your closer circle of family and friends appreciate your views simply because those interpretations complement their ideals.

## Brand magnitude

This represents brand supremacy in terms of esteem rather than pure apportion within a market sector.

In terms of your reinvention, this can be measured by the genuine admiration which you inspire in others. Not simply because of how well known you have become through publicity, self-generated or otherwise, but specifically the respect and regard that people have for your integrity.

## Brand affinity

The allegiance and admiration the brand attracts from existing as well as potential customers.

Again, in terms of your reinvention, how emotionally involved your immediate family, friends and acquaintances feel towards you. Of even greater significance, the strength of connection felt by others when learning of your personal beliefs, values and vision. Providing that allegiance is strong enough, people will be happy to speak highly of your reputation.

## Brand sensitivity

This can be summed up as the feelings and emotions evoked by the brand.

In terms of your reinvention, this equates with your temperament. Depending on the honesty, consistency and frankness of your reinvention, so people will want to be associated with everything you represent and embody through direct action, rather than superficial pledges.

## Reinventors do it inside out

There is a kind of branding technique called, 'bumper sticker strategy'. This is when a company summarizes its brand's meaning in a memorable one-line phrase, rather like the slogans you may put in the back window of your car. A great bumper sticker strategy shows a clear competitive difference. It offers shareholders a tangible promise. It encourages employees' customers. It underpins an organization's strategy and core competencies.

Imagine that you were asked to design your own bumper sticker strategy to place on the back window of your car. In no more than seven words, it would have to explain your values, competencies and individuality. What would those words be?

## Cracking the brand

In one of my books, *Teach Yourself Imaginative Marketing* (Hodder Headline) I discuss something called 'the brand egg'. Just as an egg perfectly contains the mainstay ingredients for life, so 'the brand egg' features the essential elements of a powerful brand.

The yolk represents the brand's core strengths; the white its supporting values. The shell, its external face to the public, so the first impressions that are presented by a professional branding campaign.

That 'egg' is part of your own life make-up. How you present it depends on you. In whichever way you decide to brand your reinvention, I trust the results will turn out 'sunny side up', rather than scrambled.

- To be enduring, present a definitive set of identifiable values.

- Don't just practise what you preach, learn how to understand yourself even better and then teach others to practise their own beliefs.

- The power of any brand or reinvention project is only as sturdy as its substance.

- Aim to be an original rather than 'me-too'.

- Everyone is looking for someone to believe in. Look to yourself.

- Why just aim to be 'quite good'? Strive to become 'the best'.

- You are – therefore you do.

- Assimilate your values into everyday life.

- When you are committed to reinvention, that commitment encourages people to feel obligated to you.

- Make reinvention inspirationally simple.

- Take small steps to improve continuously.

- The more you involve people, the more they will want to be drawn in.

- Don't mistake 'character' for 'resilience'.

- Don't follow stereotypes.

- Be careful: unfulfilled promises engender unforgiving adversaries.

- In a world led by choice, make your first choice *you for the benefit of all.*

- ◆ If you have to reinvent your reinvention – do it.

- ◆ Just as a great brand 'lives' its pledge, so you should 'live' your ideals.

- ◆ However you measure success, make sure it's not so high that you can't reach your goals.

# chapter ten
## fit defence

reinvent yourself

momentum

Much of what I have discussed has been aimed at your adopting the right attitude of mind. Yet, to activate your thoughts you also need to keep fit physically, mentally and emotionally.

Fitness trainer and counsellor, Michael Levene, explains that unless you care for your body, lethargy can creep in and ultimately you could simply ground to a halt.

Fitness which helps focus on reinventing yourself can relieve much of the pressures arising from everyday stress. In his book, *The Games People Play*, Eric Berne explains that a person begins life as a 'free child'. That means having the freedom to say aloud what is felt within. Over the child's formative years, parents may try to repress many of those feelings. For example cautioning a curious child to '*Stop saying that man has a big nose, it's rude*'. The child takes note of these directives and by the age of seven develops into the 'adaptive child'.

In many instances, by the time children mature into adolescence and later adulthood, they generally tend to incorporate their repressed feelings into everyday working life. This generates stress, which in turn calls for some kind of outlet. Some may turn to drink, others to meditation, uppers, downers, sex, eating, smoking (legal or illegal), gambling or whatever foible gets them through the day, and more crucially, night. If they put their mind to it, most can turn to fitness.

Michael continues:

If left unchecked, stress may lead to depression. [According to the British Health and Safety Executive, workplace stress accounts for around six million absentee days per year.] Many managers or would-be managers cringe when they hear the 'D' word. In the working world, the 'D' word can be acknowledged as a badge of honour worn by an individual believing in sacrificing everything for the greater good of the company. On the other hand, the 'D' word can symbolize weakness. I think that depression, especially depression arising from feeling powerless to make the necessary commitment towards trying to reinvent oneself, serves as the body's secondary warning system (the first being stress). Unless depression is treated, ideally through counselling, the entire emotional system could suffer a breakdown.

Many believe in the sway of life scripts – the values or otherwise drummed into a child's mind up until the age of seven, after which he or she becomes the 'adaptive child'. Those values are often implanted through good intention but end up leaving long-term damage. For example, most parents want their kids to succeed at school so, in an attempt to encourage them, they say something like, 'I know you are going to fail, now prove me wrong'. The child then approaches schoolwork from a negative stance. Every effort becomes a gigantic task.

Invariably such children grow up maintaining that negative outlook on life, convincing themselves that whatever they attempt, say at work, from filing to sales will probably fail – but they go ahead anyway. Many even seek out employers who reaffirm those inner feelings:

'Check out the artwork on this project – you'll probably miss quite a lot of mistakes – but as a "good manager" it's my duty to offer you the chance to learn.'

When it comes to the same people who use fitness programmes to remain absorbed on reinvention, they may think 'I know I am going to fail at keep fit and I am going to prove my instincts are right.'

## You – only leaner

Fit Defence is concerned with managing yourself and your personal space to become fitter and more confident. Unlike many other exercise techniques, it is based on the plausible rather than possible.

Michael takes up the story:

Rather than put yourself under the strain of even going as far as to join a fitness centre, initially your only commitment is to set aside even a very small amount of time in your day for exercise. Fitness changes don't need to be drastic. For example, instead of catching the bus all the way to work, step off one or two stops before your usual disembarkation point. Or walk the dog. Or instead of driving to the shops, cycle there. Once you feel comfortable with these small steps, you can progress further. For those who are wealthy enough, that may include joining the gym, which in itself doesn't necessarily resolve any long-term issues of fitness.

The best gym of all is your environment. For press-ups, use park benches. For endurance, jog to your local high street and back. For weight training, lift heavily laden boxes (with caution). For cardiovascular training, run up and down a staircase, thirty times. As long as you check first with your doctor and balance the amount of exercise taken with the amount of food eaten, you will notice great results.

## Know your limits – then cheat.

There comes a stage in all forms of exercise when the body reaches a certain limit of fitness and then levels itself out. This is a danger point for anyone wishing to push training intensity further still. This limitation is called 'adaptation'. If you are not careful, it could lead to actually gaining weight – so you become a fitter, yet fatter person! To counteract this, you have to out-smart adaptation. To 'trick' it, vary your exercise programme until your body adapts to new levels of success.

Michael encourages would-be reinventors to record over an initial two-week period everything they eat. This lets you see first hand just how much 'input' you are taking and then compare it to a second chart showing exercise 'output'. Providing you keep to recommended daily calories for men and women, this exercise could be quite an eye opener in itself. And once you start to *feel* fit, you can begin to *act* fit both in mind and body.

### Take the lead

The media encourage people to pay a great deal of attention to their diet. However, sometimes they do so at the risk of overlooking the importance of paying equal attention to their minds.

Stressed-out reinventors looking for a little bit of peace and tranquillity could find relief through simple hypnosis and meditation. For example, closing your eyes and taking deep breaths.

Michael continues:

One of the best techniques is to count every two breaths taken as one. Do this until you count up to 25. Invariably, by the time you reach nine, your mind will stray and you'll find it difficult to keep a tally of your count. However, the more you practise, the better you'll become and the calmer too.

When you alter your state of consciousness, you get in touch with your autonomic nervous system. This deals with managing issues like your heart rate and hormone balance. Meditation taps into this subconscious where you also retain your memories and feelings.

Through quietly programming yourself, you can prevent your subconscious from becoming your programmer. It's all a matter of control and taking the lead over your own actions. Once you gain control, you can call the shots. (*Also see* 'Re-program your head'.)

Think of it like this: often people who have reinvention thrust upon them, rather than it being the result of their own actions, find themselves at a loss on how best to handle their feelings towards change. For example, someone who wins the lottery may suddenly wonder what to do all day, now that they don't have to work. This may sound like a problem worth having, however, once you take away hunger, there's no longer much fun having unlimited access to a sweet shop. Feelings, initiative and enterprise all get muddled up.

Even more commonly, people who reach middle age owning their own house and car, bringing up a family, as well as having accomplished their career ambitions, may well wonder what to do next. Moreover, how to recapture their inner energy to get all fired-up about the prospect.

Clearly, as part of an overall plan, keeping fit in both the mind and body allows you as a reinventor to set goals and train yourself to progress purposefully through life, rather than wander aimlessly gaining weight and losing direction in the empty hope of stumbling on opportunity which may or may not arise.

- Set realistic goals.

- Manage your time to accommodate those goals.

- Record what you eat and even more importantly, how much exercise you undertake. (Simply seeing what you have achieved, however modest, can lead to even greater achievements.)

- Carry with you any feelings of accomplishment.

- Every commitment you make to exercise is subconsciously directed at the fulfilment of your wider reinvention goals. (In other words – success – however modest – breeds success).

- If you suffer a set-back, re-visit your charts. Remember you can always carry yourself further.

- If you aim to be fitter, failure is not the worst thing in the world. The very worst is not to try in the fist place.

- Yo-yo dieting can never replace you, you confidence.

- While you can become learner on the outside never try to shed a gram of who you are on the inside.

- One of the most rewarding exercises is to take 15 exercising your mind.

- Freedom starts by feeling liberated within.

- Control, like any aspect of reinvention, is yours for the taking.

- 'Knock-knock who's there? – opportunity', is a joke. In reality, opportunity seldom knocks twice, so keep your door open.

- Getting 'it' wrong shows you how to get it right.

reinvent yourself

# chapter eleven
## great to see you again

reinvent yourself

momentum

By now, you should be feeling pretty confident about your reinvention prospects. It's time to tell the world of your achievements. You have heard of the saying, 'It's not *what* you know, it's *who* you know that matters.' That adage is an integral part of reinvention.

Everything you do in your life is somehow interconnected. With the right connections, your reinvention can go further than you would have dreamt possible. The quandary is just finding those connections.

Look no further than your immediate circle of friends – and even more importantly, *acquaintances*. List out every friend you have gained in the last five years. I regard a 'friend' as someone whom you have been out with socially, say for a drink, on more than two occasions. Next look down at your list and highlight the people who originally introduced you to your wider circle of friends. Finally, group the friends and the people they introduced you to in different clusters.

To discover the strongest links, identify those people who provided you with the most friends through their introductions. To establish the most influential, and so powerful links, identify further those who provided you with the most introductions.

Your aim is to become a link that doesn't simply know the most people but the best contacts that know other people across lots of different groups.

When looking for a job, perhaps one that best matches your reinvented self, you will probably speak to head-hunters or check the newspapers and the Web for vacancies or write to companies or even ask friends to introduce you to the right connectors.

Yet, when it comes down to it, you'll probably find that rather than friends who 'live' in your 'world' and so hang around with the same people as you, the best connectors are in fact your acquaintances. These people occasionally 'step cross' over to your 'world' but also 'live' and mix in other circles. Pinpointing such acquaintances calls for 'getting out there', joining as many organizations as possible and meeting people.

## Tuesday's child is full of grace

When the dot coms were booming rather than exploding, a club was started for Netrepreneurs called, 'First Tuesday'. It was usually held at some local trendy wine bar on the first Tuesday of every month. The meetings comprised two main types of groups, namely those with bright ideas for new dot com ventures and investors.

As you would expect, there would be brighter ideas from the 'ideas' people in attendance than from investors. As the dotE-conomy slumped, so the number of investors dwindled. It all became so ridiculous that at some local UK meetings, the only people to bump into were those looking for investors. In other words, everyone was going around in ever decreasing circles!

Just as you have to stay ahead by being prepared to move into awkward yet potentially rewarding new spheres, so without forsaking really great friends, you'll find that it pays to venture into new circles of acquaintances. (Providing, of course, that you can add some value to each new circle – no one likes a hanger-on!) Once you have established yourself across your key circles, you will become one of the powerful links which others will be eager to be associated with.

Now, as a *powerful link,* you can begin to influence others rather than just live in hope that others will one day listen to you. What if you want to persuade a specific circle of people about your ideas? Then know who within that circle wields the greatest influence over his or her peers.

For example, let's say you have designed a new type of fashion accessory that promises to reinvent the essence of 'cool'. You need to get the accessory talked about by those 'in the know' within the world (circle) of fashion.

# Adopt a geek.

I would suggest that you adopt a geek. A geek is someone at the cutting edge of his or her social, working – or in this case, fashion circle. In the field of marketing, such a person would be called an 'Innovator'; a categorization first coined by Everett Rogers in 1962.

- ◆ *Innovators* are always open minded to reinventors. If you can convince them of your ideas, they will convince other people ('Early Adopters' – see below) within their circle.

- ◆ *Early Adopters* comprise a much larger group who are keen to be admired as being trendy by their peers, including contemporaries from different 'circles'. Innovators and Early Adopters together make up around 20 per cent of the total number in any particular group. Yet, thanks to their visionary ways of recognizing what's in and what's not, they influence 80 per cent of the total circle.

Once Early Adopters have taken to an idea, they go out to convince a group divided into two sub-sections, namely, the Early and Late Majorities.

- ◆ *Late* and *Early Majority* are sceptics, only taking up a reinvented concept if it has undergone some kind of testing procedure and through doing so, has met with general all-round approval. Thanks to the Early Adopters and Innovators, it has.

The final group constitutes the largest one, specifically, the laggards.

◆ *Laggards* only adopt an idea once they really have no other option. Thanks to your collaboration, with just about everyone else in the group taking up the idea, they will feel obliged to follow suit.

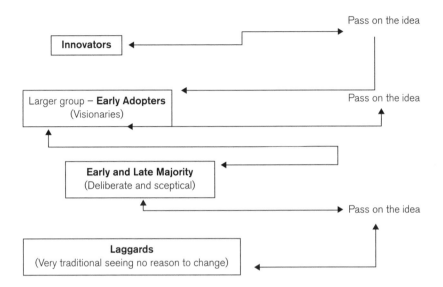

## When is advertising not advertising?

Many of the world's most successful companies don't use traditional advertising to spread their message. Instead, they work on the power of networking between key players. Instead of placing expensive ads, which may or may not be read, and thereafter may or not be answered, and thereafter may or not convert into a solid sale, powerful companies market their products or services through establishing strong connections.

For example, a business consultancy may regularly publish articles, brochures or even books. It may send out emails relating to interesting developments, which may appeal to existing and potential clients. It may also publish a regular magazine or similar

Web-distributed 'e-zine' circulated to existing as well as old clients and staff, keeping them informed of future schemes. In return, those contacts bear in mind the consultancy for future projects or joint ventures. Providing the consultancy stays in circulation, so word of mouth about them also goes round the profession.

In terms of publishing, you could follow suit. For example, writing articles for your trade magazines. (My experience in public relations taught me that many such magazines are always looking for talented reinventors with bright ideas.) Taking up the 'e-zine' idea, you could keep in touch with former acquaintances via simple html formatted email, perhaps pointing them to an amusing or pertinent article which you came across on the Web.

Encourage former contacts to share your thoughts on new product developments in your industry sector. The key is to keep your name circulating around the industry – for the right reasons. When the time arises to find the right person for an important task – and it will – your name will be the first to call.

## What goes around, comes around

Keeping in touch with key players can also mean being part of a wider circle of contacts, such as belonging to charitable, trade and cultural organizations. Again, once the word gets around, your reputation will grow. Who knows, you might even become the next 'keynote' speaker at an important event. That will put you in front of even more influential people, who in turn will speak highly of you to others … So your network gets larger.

**The wider your name is spread, the greater your 'share of mind' over the people you are targeting.**

As with all reinvention techniques, you don't have to be a major conglomerate to make an impact. Perhaps you could get a spot on a local radio – as 'the expert in … '

- Maybe you could speak to a chamber of commerce about offering consultancy services to businesses looking for your kind of experience.

- Maybe you could run your own seminar or presentation at lunchtime for local business people.

- Maybe you could offer an initial free consultancy, leading to further opportunities later.

- Maybe you could approach someone who has made the headlines, detailing either how you could help take their success even further, or providing a useful different angle on matters. (Just speak to the journalist who wrote the article, or the headline maker's own PR people. Alternatively, write a letter – or better still, call them direct – reinventors dare to tread where others simply dread.)

- Maybe you could join key networking clubs whose relevancy is still appropriate for today's needs.

The opportunities are as long as the names of contacts in your local Yellow Pages. There's no end to the number of people who want to make the headlines or who are looking to reinvent themselves or their businesses and would value your talent to help them succeed.

## Who says you can't judge a book by its cover?

The key is to relay your reinvented idea and enthusiasm into the minds and hearts of the right people. Earlier I referred to my book, *Teach Yourself Copywriting* (Hodder Headline). I was determined to ensure that the book would be adopted by the advertising industry *en bloc*, but wasn't quite sure how to go about it.

During the course of my work, I would attend meetings at various advertising agencies. Invariably I noticed that company directors had a shelf containing a few books about advertising practice. Funnily enough, the more prestigious or 'wacky' the book-bindings, the greater the prominence on the shelf.

Acting on the evidence, I negotiated with my publisher to buy at cost one thousand copies of my book. I then asked a designer to re-cover the book in a special binding and insert it in a bespoke presentation case, which could be mailed.

After that it was simply a matter of choosing one thousand key 'influencers' to whom I could send copies, which slowly but surely landed on bookcases. And so whenever someone asked the 'influencer' for a good book about copywriting or for some independent copywriting advice, in most cases my book was recommended. Today, the book has been adopted by the world's biggest marketing institute as key reading for students wishing to learn about copywriting. It remains a best seller.

## Take a note Ms Jones

A similar story affected the highly popular 'Post It Notes' manufactured by 3M. When launched, the product was a failure.

# Initially, no one could identify a real need for a piece of paper with tacky glue on the back.

Then a senior director from 3M – listed on the Fortune 500 as one of America's foremost companies – decided to send a carton of Post It Notes to each of the remaining 499 companies. The cartons were addressed to the secretaries of the chairpersons.

The secretaries started to use and circulate the Post It Notes around their offices. Correspondents began to notice the little oblong notes attached to letters and reports and asked where they too could get hold of the little memo stickers. And the rest, as they say, is history.

It was an ingenious illustration of how through connecting directly with the kind of people who benefit directly from new ideas – in this case secretaries – a reinventor can spread them quickly, effectively and cheaply.

# Spreading reinvention further still

Once you establish whom to target with your reinvented ideas, the next step is to break down your target audience into very discrete sectors. These discrete segments will probably fall within the Early and Late Majority part of the circles that I discussed earlier. By winning over the hearts and minds of these highly targeted audiences, you'll find that as you conquer each macro market, your success automatically gains pace with the next market segment, as outlined in the diagram.

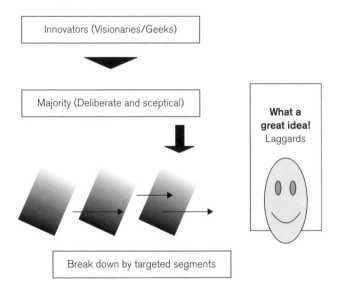

'Rising above the noise of a thousand voices requires creativity.'

Steve Jurvetson, venture capitalist for Hotmail

Both currently and in the future, the Web offers people a direct route to finding what they need. So if, for example, you are going to use the Web to publish your CV, which reflects your reinvented self, you should take into consideration aspects such as:

◆ How quickly potential employers can navigate around your site.

◆ The clarity of your message – using simple, but not condescending language.

- The originality of your site design – reflecting the originality of your thinking.

- The simplicity of your communication – people want to get to the core of your message quickly.

- The value of its content – for example, are you using the site to help people gain up-to-date information about your projects?

- The 'stickiness' of your site – are you offering something that will give people a reason to return to the site – time after time?

- Your site's ability to act as a contagious transmitter – are you offering something as simple as an apt and witty 'thought of the day' that will encourage people to forward your message?

- Your site's unambiguous relevance to key influencers.

- The ease for such VIPs to access that message and then carry it further.

The easer it is to access your site, the more powerful it becomes in reaching wider and wider audiences; hence the greater your potential to influence the ideal people who can help bring your reinvention to fruition. One tried and tested way to achieve this is adding a message signature at the bottom of every email you send.

This is precisely how MSN's hotmail was first introduced to the world. A 'signature' was attached to the tail of every email sent by the company to its users. It read:

'Get Your Private, Free Email at http://www.hotmail.com'. Within 18 months, Hotmail had signed up 12 million users while spending just $500,000 on marketing.

Just as fashion followers spread new fads simply by wearing them and walking along the street – in the right neighbourhoods – so the superhighway offers a reinventor the ideal platform to spread a message not just across town, but entire continents.

Whether you are networking on the Web or in person, ensure that you make the right connections not just by being wired but through becoming connected to the people who count and who could one day soon come to count on you.

## REINVENTING YOU

◆ Every reinvention step you take is interconnected.

◆ Recognize which of your friends and acquaintances have the strongest links to a wider group of contacts.

◆ Aim to establish your own set of powerful contacts.

◆ Gain acquaintances without forsaking friends.

◆ Use the power of networking to expand your reinvention project.

◆ Reinventors dare to tread where others simply dread.

◆ Plan to gain 'share-of-mind' of your audience.

◆ Use key influencers to act as viral carriers of your reinvention.

◆ Harness the Web to tell people what they initially need to hear and thanks to your design, what offers greater relevance to their future aspirations.

◆ To infiltrate large communities, first influence small groups.

# chapter twelve
## the beginning

reinvent yourself

Just as supernovas created our planet, it is predicted that the ferocity of the sun will eventually destroy earth and, like all other stars, ultimately itself. In so doing a new-born star may rekindle the process of life all over again.

Just as in the infancy of evolution when through adaptation and ingenuity, man stood on two feet, the next development of mankind may even adapt its anatomy to thrive in environments considered today as hostile.

## The beauty of reinvention is that it's the art of the possible.

The core process of reinvention has little to do with what you make. It has more to do with what you make of *yourself*. It takes strength and courage not just to stay ahead of the reinvention race for success, but to leap over the occasional hurdles that you may encounter as part of life's marathon.

In bringing this book to a close, I'll leave you with a thought from my 10-year-old son, Joshua, as well as an aptly inspirational true story.

I was giving Joshua a lift to school. On listening to yet another radio report about the atrocities of war and terrorism, he asked one of those impossible 'son-to-dad' questions: 'Why did all those innocent people have to die?'

I bit my lip before responding. 'Maybe if those people hadn't gone through all that terrible suffering, history would have taken a very different course. I guess the world would have turned out to be very different. Sometimes things don't make sense. Yet, over a period of time, maybe a very, very long time, it somehow all falls into place.' Joshua glanced out of the window. 'Does that mean that those people were meant to suffer?' The conversation was getting far too deep for a normal lift to school. I fell into an awkward silence.

At the school gate, Joshua waved goodbye, then turned and walked back to the car. I rolled down the passenger window. 'Maybe Dad', he said, 'life is really best enjoyed when you know you have really done your best. I suppose if you treat people as *you* would want to be treated – *the very best way* – every one comes out smiling.'

Maybe the kid's right!

My only sister, Brenda, is in her mid-forties, married with two children. A few years ago she was struck down by multiple sclerosis. It led her to being virtually bed-ridden in a nursing home with little, if any, prospect of a cure.

I visit her regularly. Despite her debilitating health, I cannot help but admire Brenda's remarkable efforts to bring a smile to the face of all her carers and visitors. Such a courageous response to look ahead with confidence rather than back in anger has inspired me throughout the writing of this book.

The nature of Progressive Secondary MS can mean that the patient can lose short-term memory. A technique to stimulate them is simply to repeat a phrase, which can be associated with an event or person. The opening epigram to Shirley Conran's 1975 book *Superwoman* was 'Life's too short to stuff a mushroom'. Drawing on this, I plucked the phrase, 'life is too short for peeling carrots'. On the surface, quite a silly statement, but it worked, and even now my sister associates it with my daft ways. So much so that sometimes she repeats it back to me!

Recently as she spoke, something particularly striking about those words occurred to me. Perhaps when it comes to reinvention and all it entails, including being for yourself when others are not, planning success, understanding roles at work, assertion, networking and pushing towards limits that you would had previously considered impossible, reinvention comes down to just getting on with it. Rather than settling for peeling layers upon identical layers of your life, do what you hanker after by pushing for what you deserve.

Echoing the sentiments of a song by Sting:

Turn the clock to zero boss
The river's wide, we'll swim across
We're starting up a brand new day ...

It's time for you to start thinking in a brand new way. In your attempt to reinvent yourself you'll probably make mistakes (as will I). But that's okay. As the world's first space tourist, Dennis Tito, said, 'When you don't know where you are going to end up, you focus on your journey and that carries you forward.'

As you close this, the final page of the book, muster the strength and courage to make a fresh and determined start on reinvention – your reinvention. Wherever you end doesn't matter, providing that on every step of your journey you can count your blessings for you being *you*.

jj@gabaynet.com

reinvent yourself